CEFR-J
A2.2–B2.2

Thinking About Our Future

Learning About the SDGs in English

Paul Gregory Quinn
Yoshiyuki Okaura

SANSHUSHA

音声ダウンロード＆ストリーミングサービス（無料）のご案内

https://www.sanshusha.co.jp/text/onsei/isbn/9784384335163/

本書の音声データは、上記アドレスよりダウンロードおよびストリーミング再生ができます。ぜひご利用ください。

Download

Streaming

The content of this publication has not been approved by the United Nations and does not reflect the views of the United Nations or its officials or Member States.

photo:

SDG 1	Dennis Diatel/Shutterstock.com
SDG 2	PreciousPhotos/Shutterstock.com
SDG 3	REDPIXEL.PL/Shutterstock.com
SDG 4	Boxed Lunch Productions/Shutterstock.com
SDG 5	Blick/Shutterstock.com
SDG 6	Tatevosian Yana/Shutterstock.com
SDG 7	SAHAN1_1/Shutterstock.com
SDG 8	Jacob Lund/Shutterstock.com
SDG 9	Bannafarsai_Stock/Shutterstock.com
SDG 10	Hyejin Kang/Shutterstock.com
SDG 11	Catalin Lazar/Shutterstock.com
SDG 12	HalynaRom/Shutterstock.com
SDG 13	Scott Book/Shutterstock.com
SDG 14	Ethan Daniels/Shutterstock.com
SDG 15	Milan Zygmunt/Shutterstock.com
SDG 16	All for you friend/Shutterstock.com
SDG 17	Chinnapong/Shutterstock.com

Preface

What are the advantages of using this textbook? You will get a good understanding of the 17 United Nations' (UN) Sustainable Development Goals (SDGs) while also developing your English reading, listening, writing, and speaking abilities.

The SDGs show what the UN aims to achieve for our planet by the year 2030. Learning about the SDGs is important because they are regularly in the news, often influence government policy, and may affect every person on Earth. Each unit of this textbook uses a short reading passage to explain one SDG in English that is easy to understand, describing what that goal is, providing reasons why it is needed, and indicating how the UN wants to achieve that SDG. That reading passage is followed by a student and professor dialogue that explores the details of that SDG in more depth, using the kind of authentic English that is rarely found in textbooks.

Another reason that you should choose this textbook is that it can help improve your English reading, speaking, listening, and writing. The book is designed to help you become a more fluent reader by increasing your English vocabulary and your ability to guess the meaning of unknown vocabulary through context (or the words around that vocabulary). It also provides practice in answering main idea, detail, and opinion questions, which are designed to improve your reading and listening comprehension skills and provide important practice in English writing and speaking. The three-step active listening process used in this textbook helps you to improve your listening comprehension ability through prediction, confirmation, and reflection. Furthermore, this textbook regularly engages you in the kind of challenging oral and written production that increases communicative ability and creates multiple opportunities for corrective feedback.

We would like to thank our families for being patient with our absences as we wrote this textbook. Furthermore, we are quite grateful to the wonderful people at Sanshusha. We received helpful suggestions and support from them, and we truly appreciated the extended deadlines we got when we needed them. Moreover, we wish to thank our institutions, Centennial College and Fukuoka Institute of Technology, for our employment, and also the University of Toronto, where we met and began collaborating with each other on several educational endeavours. It is also important to state how grateful we are for the UN SDG website https://www.un.org/sustainabledevelopment/ that provided the information about the SDGs which we used to create *Thinking About Our Future: Learning About the SDGs in English*. Finally, we are most thankful to you for choosing this textbook, which we are confident will be an excellent resource for learning about the SDGs while learning English.

Paul Gregory Quinn, PhD and Professor Yoshiyuki Okaura, Toronto, Canada, July 15, 2022

How to Use This Textbook

This textbook covers all 17 SDGs by dedicating a unit to each one. The units can be studied in order. However, the units are designed to stand alone, so you can study as many units as you wish, in whatever order you want. Each unit follows the same structure, which goes through a series of sections that are explained below.

INTRODUCTION

Each unit starts with the name and number of the SDG that it covers along with the UN's official symbol for that SDG and a photograph that illustrates what that SDG is about. On that photograph, there are two questions. The purpose of the first question is to encourage you to use what you already know about the topic to predict what the SDG is about. The second question requires you to use creative thinking to draw your own symbol for the SDG and explain how your version compares with the UN's official symbol.

VOCABULARY

The Vocabulary section pre-teaches seven essential words from the unit's reading passage. Pre-teaching these words is a vocabulary building task. In addition, it helps you understand the reading passage by allowing you to think about the meaning of the passage without being distracted by unknown vocabulary. Not only that but working with these seven words will help you to predict what the reading passage is about.

In the first part of this section, you listen to the definitions of the seven words and fill in the words that are missing in the definitions. For example, in Unit 1, you will hear the definition of housing as "A place to live, such as an apartment or a house" and fill in the blanks with "live, such as."

In the second part, you must use the contextual clues (or hints about the word's meaning that are around the word) in the example sentences to guess which word (from the square word bank under the items) is needed to fill in the blank in each item. Thus, for the first item "A. Coca-Cola is an _____ beverage. You can buy it many countries." you can guess the correct word is "international" because an adjective is required and the second sentence includes "many countries," which is a synonym to "international." Practice in guessing a word by the context will make you a better reader over time.

READING

The Reading section begins with three questions designed to continue the process of prediction about the passage that began in the Vocabulary section. Anticipating what will be read in a passage increases your comprehension. You should then read the text to discover whether your answers were correct or not.

The reading passage itself is structured in the same way in all units. Getting used to that structure will help you to read the passages more fluently as you go through the units. There are two paragraphs. The first paragraph explains what the Unit's SDG is about and why it is something that the UN wants to address before 2030. The second paragraph tells you some of the important things the UN aims at achieving to address that SDG. The seven essential words that you learned in the vocabulary section appear in blue font in the reading passage.

After reading the passage, you can once again engage in vocabulary building with the Words and Phrases activity, which further helps you to understand the reading passage. This activity includes 10 words from the passage. To complete the Words and Phrases activity, you read simple definitions of the 10 words and search the reading passage for the word or phrase that matches the definition. To help you, the number of letters in each mystery word or phrase is provided in dashes, which makes this activity like a crossword puzzle and focuses you on correct spelling as well as meaning. Both the words and the definitions in the "VOCABULARY" and "Words and Phrases" sections in this textbook begin with capital letters.

The final components of the Reading section are the two kinds of reading comprehension questions. First, there is a main idea question which is sometimes about the main idea of the entire passage and sometimes about just one paragraph of the passage. This question always provides four multiple-choice answers. The multiple-choice answers will help you avoid the common mistakes that people make when answering main idea questions on English tests. For example, sometimes there are distractors that seem like the correct answer. At other times, a detail is provided which is in the passage but is not the main idea. You can find the main idea by skimming (or reading the first and last sentence or quickly reading every other line). Sometimes, but not always, the main idea can be found in the first or last lines of a passage. However, the main idea can always be found by noticing what idea repeats throughout a passage.

Second, there are five short-answer questions about details. To answer the short-answer questions, decide what the key words are in the question. Then, scan the passage like a computer to find them. Be sure to read the area where you find the answer carefully to be certain you have found the correct details.

EXPRESS YOUR OPINION

In this section of each unit, you answer an opinion question about the unit's SDG. First, you must write your answer to the question on your own. Next, you must explain and discuss your answer with another person. This section helps you write about your own opinion and share it with other people. It also allows you to develop the ability to listen and understand the opinions of others.

LISTENING

As noted in the preface, each unit includes a dialogue between a student and a professor. The student is Sakura Noguchi, a Japanese student who is studying at a Canadian university. Sakura recently discovered the SDGs, and she is now considering majoring in International Development, so she can study more about the UN's goals for 2030. Before officially declaring her major, Sakura wants to learn more about the SDGs, so she turns to two professors in the area, Nina Jang and Alister Swain, who are experts on the SDGs. Sakura meets with these professors many times to discuss and ask questions about the SDGs.

Sakura
Noguchi

Nina
Jang

Alister
Swain

The English in the dialogues is authentic conversational English designed to help you develop your comprehension of genuine spoken English.

This textbook uses a three-step listening process, which means that you have a reason for listening each of the times that you listen to the same dialogue.

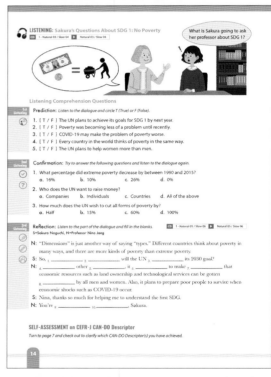

1st Listening

The first step of the listening process is called Prediction. At the top of the page, there is a question that asks you to predict what Sakura is going to ask her professor about in terms of the unit's SDG. You should actively listen to check if you were correct or not. You should also read the five True (T) or False (F) statements, so that you can circle T or F as you listen to the dialogue for the first time.

2nd Listening

The second step is called Confirmation (or making sure). In this step, you should listen so that you can check with yourself to confirm that you heard the information in the dialogue correctly. You should compare what you heard in terms of what you had predicted and also check your answer to the five T or F questions. Before listening for the second time, based on what you heard in the first listening, you should also the three multiple-choice questions, as well.

When comparing your answers to the T or F questions and trying to answer the multiple-choice questions, you should write a question mark next to any questions that you are not sure are correct. Then focus your listening on the answers with the question marks and listen again.

The third step is called Reflection. In this step, you must listen and read the excerpt from the dialogue at the same time. You should fill in the missing words.

Also, you should underline any parts of the transcript that you can understand by reading but could not catch by listening alone. After several units, you should use these underlined parts to look for patterns of weakness in your listening and then try to improve your listening in those areas that need development.

Finally, you should circle any new words and later add them (and their definitions) to the vocabulary list that you should keep.

After you have completed the three-step listening process, you should use the dialogue to practice your pronunciation. The listening section features authentic English, and you can improve how natural your English sounds by working with a partner and reading the roles in the dialogue. First, one person should read the professor's lines while the other reads Sakura's part. Then, switch roles and read the dialogue again.

Listening Speed

A very useful feature of this textbook is the listening-speed option. The dialogues are available at slow and natural speeds. You may wish to do the first two steps of the three-step listening process two times, first at the slow speed and then again at the natural speed.

SELF-ASSESSMENT on CEFR-J CAN-DO Descriptor

Some questions of this textbook are based on the CEFR-J, the Japanese version developed from the original CEFR (Common European Framework of Reference). The questions and the CEFR-J CAN-DO Descriptor and its level corresponding to them are as shown below, so after learning about each SDG through the questions, you should check out to clarify which CAN-DO Descriptors(s) you have achieved or you have not achieved.

理解（聞くこと）　UNDERSTANDING (Listening)

First Listening and Second Listening (Slow speed): B1.1
☐ I can understand the main points of extended discussions around me, provided speech is clearly articulated and in a familiar accent.

First Listening and Second Listening (Natural speed): B2.2
☐ I can understand the speaker's point of view about topics of current common interest and in specialized fields, provided it is delivered at a natural speed and articulated in standard English.

理解（読むこと）　UNDERSTANDING (Reading)

Main Idea Questions: B1.1
☐ I can understand the main points of English newspaper and magazine articles adapted for educational purposes.

Detail Questions: B2.2
☐ I can search through rather complex texts (e.g., articles and reports), and can identify key passages. I can adapt my reading speed and style, and read accurately, when I decide closer study is worthwhile.

話すこと（発表）　SPEAKING (Spoken production)

EXPRESS YOUR OPINION 1: B1.1
☐ I can talk about familiar topics and other topics of personal interest without causing confusion to the listeners, provided I can prepare my ideas in advance and use brief notes to help me.

話すこと（やりとり）　SPEAKING (Spoken interaction)

EXPRESS YOUR OPINION 1: B1.1
☐ I can express opinions and exchange information about familiar topics (e.g., school, hobbies, hopes for the future), using a wide range of simple English.

書くこと（書くこと）　WRITING (Writing)

EXPRESS YOUR OPINION 1: A2.2
☐ I can write my impressions and opinions briefly about what I have listened to and read (e.g., explanations about lifestyles, culture, stories), using basic everyday vocabulary and expressions.

---

* 『CEFR-J Version 1 (English)』CEFR-J 研究開発チーム（代表：投野由紀夫）.
（URL: http://www.cefr-j.org/download.html#cefrj より 2022 年 2 月ダウンロード）

Contents

SDG 1: No Poverty

INTRODUCTION

1. What do you think the first Sustainable Development Goal (SDG) of No Poverty is about?
2. Draw a different image to represent this SDG. Explain your image and compare it to the United Nations' official image.

VOCABULARY CD 1-01 ▶ 01

Listen to the essential words to SDGs and their definitions, and fill in each blank with the words you hear.

1. Housing (n): A place to _____, _____ _____ an apartment or a house
2. Medicine (n): A _____ or _____ used to make you _____ _____ when you are _____
3. Especially (adv): More than _____, or particularly the _____
4. Poor (adj): To have very _____ _____
5. Survive (v): To live _____ a very difficult and _____ _____
6. Quicken (v): To make something go _____
7. International (adj): Applying to _____ _____ _____ country

Fill in the blanks with the correct words below.

A. Coca-Cola is an _____ beverage. You can buy it in many countries.
B. After she lost her job, she had almost no money. She was very _____.
C. We can _____ this job if we all work together and we don't take any breaks.
D. We were lucky to _____ the earthquake, but our house was destroyed.
E. I have a headache. Do you have any _____?
F. In life, people need food, clothing, and _____.
G. Japan is _____ beautiful in the spring when the cherry blossoms bloom.

housing   medicine   especially   poor   survive   quicken   international

READING

Q1. What examples of poverty do you think you will read about in the reading?

Q2. Do you think poverty is a big problem in the world right now?

Q3. What do you think the UN plans to do about poverty?

SDG 1: No Poverty

CD 1-02 ▶ 02

The first Sustainable Development Goal (SDG) is "No Poverty." Poverty means not having enough money to pay for the basic things in life, such as food, **housing**, clothing, and **medicine**. The UN describes extreme poverty as living on less than $1.25 per day. From 1990 to 2015, the number of people living in extreme poverty went from 36% to 10%. However, today more than 10% of the

5 world's population lives in extreme poverty, and COVID-19 could cause an 8% addition in extreme poverty. There is more poverty in the countryside than in cities. (Sub-Saharan Africa is **especially poor**, and that is where the most people live who **survive** on $1.90 per day.) One out of five children in the world lives in extreme poverty. Finally, 8% of workers also live in extreme poverty.

By 2030, the UN has several targets to work on to achieve the first SDG. These targets include

10 ending extreme poverty and cutting by 50% all dimensions of poverty as they are understood by different nations. Also, the UN wants all men and women to have the same rights to economic resources and services, including land ownership, natural resources, and technological and financial services. In addition, it plans on improving poor people's ability to survive economic shocks. Furthermore, the UN wants to increase national and **international** investment to **quicken** the end of

15 poverty. The UN plans on helping to get resources and start programs to meet that goal.

Words and Phrases

Read each definition and find the equivalent word used in the Passage above.

1.	S _ _ _ _ _ _ _ _ _ _	Something can continue to work correctly for a long time
2.	D _ _ _ _ _ _ _ _ _ _	The process of becoming improved or becoming better
3.	P _ _ _ _ _ _	The state of being poor
4.	E _ _ _ _ _ _	Furthest from the middle
5.	E _ _ _ _ _ _ _	Related to the making, buying, and selling of goods and services
6.	R _ _ _ _ _ _ _ s	All the sources of wealth of a country
7.	T _ _ _ _ _ _ _ _ _ _ _	Having to do with machines
8.	F _ _ _ _ _ _ _ _	Having to do with money
9.	I _ _ _ _ _ _ _ _ _	Using money in such a way as to get a profit from it
10.	C _ _ _ _ _ _ _	The things we wear to cover our bodies, which keep us warm and protect us from the wind, rain, and sun

Main Idea   Q.   What is the main idea of the first paragraph?

      a.   To describe the UN's plans for ending poverty

      b.   To explain what happened between 1990 and 1995

      c.   To provide information about where the problem of poverty is worst

      d.   To explain why poverty is a problem

Details   1.   What does SDG stand for?

_____

    2.   How much money per day is extreme poverty?

_____

    3.   What percentage of people live in extreme poverty today?

_____

    4.   Who does the UN want to have equal rights?

_____

    5.   What is an example of an economic resource?

_____

EXPRESS YOUR OPINION

If you lived in extreme poverty for one month, what would you purchase to survive?

1. *Write your opinion and its reason concisely.*

```


```

2. *Explain your opinion and its reason concisely to your classmates.*

LISTENING: Sakura's Questions About SDG 1: No Poverty

CD 1 - Natural 03 / Slow 04 ▶ Natural 03 / Slow 04

What is Sakura going to ask her professor about SDG 1?

Listening Comprehension Questions

1st Listening

Prediction: *Listen to the dialogue and circle T (True) or F (False).*

1. [T / F] The UN plans to achieve its goals for SDG 1 by next year.
2. [T / F] Poverty was becoming less of a problem until recently.
3. [T / F] COVID-19 may make the problem of poverty worse.
4. [T / F] Every country in the world thinks of poverty in the same way.
5. [T / F] The UN plans to help women more than men.

2nd Listening

Confirmation: *Try to answer the following questions and listen to the dialogue again.*

1. What percentage did extreme poverty decrease by between 1990 and 2015?
   a. 16%   **b.** 10%   **c.** 26%   **d.** 0%

2. Who does the UN want to raise money?
   a. Companies   **b.** Individuals   **c.** Countries   **d.** All of the above

3. How much does the UN wish to cut all forms of poverty by?
   a. Half   **b.** 15%   **c.** 60%   **d.** 100%

3rd Listening

Reflection: *Listen to the part of the dialogue and fill in the blanks.*   CD 1 - Natural 05 / Slow 06 ▶ Natural 05 / Slow 06

S=Sakura Noguchi, N=Professor Nina Jang

N: "Dimensions" is just another way of saying "types." Different countries think about poverty in many ways, and there are more kinds of poverty than extreme poverty.

S: So, 1. _____ 2. _____ will the UN 3. _____ its 2030 goal?

N: 4. _____ other 5. _____, it 6. _____ to make 7. _____ that economic resources such as land ownership and technological services can be gotten 8. _____ by all men and women. Also, it plans to prepare poor people to survive when economic shocks such as COVID-19 occur.

S: Nina, thanks so much for helping me to understand the first SDG.

N: You're 9. _____ 10. _____, Sakura.

SELF-ASSESSMENT on CEFR-J CAN-DO Descriptor

Turn to page 7 and determine which CAN-DO Descriptor(s) you have achieved.

SDG 2: Zero Hunger

INTRODUCTION

1. What do you think the second SDG of Zero Hunger is about?
2. Draw a different image to represent this SDG. Explain your image and compare it to the UN's official image.

VOCABULARY CD 1 - 07 ▶ 07

Listen to the essential words to SDGs and their definitions, and fill in each blank with the words you hear.

1. Healthy (adj): Good for your _____ or _____
2. Prevents (v): To _____ something from _____
3. Improvements (n): Things that _____ something to become _____
4. Production (n): The _____ of things
5. Achieve (v): To _____ a _____
6. Encouraging (v): To _____ _____ someone to do something
7. Technology (n): _____ that is made by using _____ _____

Fill in the blanks with the correct words below.

A. Japan is famous for automobile _____. Many of the best carmakers in the world are Japanese, such as Honda, Nissan, and Toyota.
B. If you want to _____ success in school, then you must study hard and often.
C. _____ such as personal computers and printers makes students' lives easier.
D. Eating _____ food that has a lot of vitamins helps you live longer.
E. The government gave our village money for better roads and other _____.
F. My friends are _____ me to join a gym to lose weight.
G. The research shows that the vaccine _____ people from getting COVID-19.

healthy   prevents   improvements   production   achieve   encouraging   technology

READING

Q1. What do you think you will read about in terms of hunger in the reading?

Q2. Do you think hunger is a big problem in the world right now?

Q3. What do you think the UN plans to do about hunger?

SDG 2: Zero Hunger

CD 1 - 08 ▶ 08

The second SDG is "Zero Hunger." The UN explains hunger in two ways. First, hunger means malnourishment, or not having enough of the right kinds of food to keep you **healthy**. Second, there is acute hunger, wherein not having enough food **prevents** people from working or causes death. Today, 820 million people suffer from daily hunger, and 135 million have acute hunger (caused by
5 wars, climate change, and economic problems). COVID-19 may cause the number of people with acute hunger to double. Global **improvements** to farming and food **production** are needed.

The UN plans to **achieve** the second SDG in several ways. By 2030, it wants to end all malnourishment and acute hunger. It hopes to double global food production and incomes of small-scale food producers such as family farmers and fishers. Also, the UN wishes to help food producers
10 improve their production by **encouraging** them to use different types of animals and plants that are better able to survive in poor conditions such as when there is too much or not enough rain. Finally, the UN wants to improve the international use of money and laws to help food producers get better **technology**, use their land better, and be able to buy and sell what they need more easily.

Words and Phrases

Read each definition and find the equivalent word used in the Passage above.

1.	S _ _ _ _ _	To experience pain or loss
2.	C _ _ _ _	To bring something about or make something happen
3.	D _ _ _ _ _	To be multiplied by two, or to be increased by 100%
4.	I _ _ _ _ _	Money that comes into an individual
5.	M _ _ _ _ _ _ _ _ _ _ _ _	Not getting enough food or the right sort of food
6.	F _ _ _ _ _ _	Using land for growing crops or raising animals
7.	P _ _ _ _ _ _ _	A farmer or manufacturer
8.	C _ _ _ _ _ _	The long-term pattern of weather
9.	H _ _ _ _ _	The state of not having enough food to eat
10.	A _ _ _ _	Serious and severe

Main Idea   Q. What is the main idea of the first paragraph?

   a. To explain that hunger results in malnourishment
   b. To explain that hunger is worse than acute hunger
   c. To explain two types of hunger that cause different problems worldwide
   d. To explain what the UN plans to do about world hunger

Details   1. How many people suffer from daily hunger?

   _____

   2. How many people may suffer from acute hunger after COVID-19?

   _____

   3. How much does the UN plan to increase food production?

   _____

   4. What else does the UN want to increase for small-scale food producers?

   _____

   5. Name one kind of small-scale food producer.

   _____

EXPRESS YOUR OPINION

If you were engaged in agriculture or fishery, how could you reduce the number of people with acute hunger?

1. *Write your opinion and its reason concisely.*

```
┌─────────────────────────────────────────────────────────┐
│                                                         │
│                                                         │
│                                                         │
│                                                         │
│                                                         │
└─────────────────────────────────────────────────────────┘
```

2. *Explain your opinion and its reason concisely to your classmates.*

CD 1 - Natural 09 / Slow 10 ▶ Natural 09 / Slow 10

> What is Sakura going to ask her professor about SDG 2?

Listening Comprehension Questions

1st Listening

Prediction: *Listen to the dialogue and circle T (True) or F (False).*

1. [T / F] This meeting happens in the morning.
2. [T / F] Sakura has met Professor Swain many times before.
3. [T / F] Sakura thinks that hunger is becoming less of a problem.
4. [T / F] Sakura is surprised by the UN's goal for 2030.
5. [T / F] The UN is going to use money to buy different plants and animals.

2nd Listening

Confirmation: *Try to answer the following questions and listen to the dialogue again.*

1. What should Sakura call the professor?
   a. Nina **b.** Mister Swain **c.** Professor Swain **d.** Alister

2. What year did hunger start increasing again?
   a. 2016 **b.** 2030 **c.** 2015 **d.** 2013

3. What does the UN plan to do about hunger?
   a. Double the amount of food production **b.** Help small-scale food producers
   c. Improve food-producing technology **d.** All of the above

3rd Listening

Reflection: *Listen to the part of the dialogue and fill in the blanks.*

CD 1 - Natural 11 / Slow 12 ▶ Natural 11 / Slow 12

S=Sakura Noguchi, A=Professor Alister Swain

A: For one thing, it wants to end hunger by 2030 by doubling the 1. _____ of food 2. _____ in the world.

S: Double? Wow!

A: Yes, and that's not all. It plans to help small-scale food producers to 3. _____ bad 4. _____ by encouraging them to use different kinds of plants and animals that are stronger.

S: What 5. _____ will the UN do?

A: It plans to use 6. _____ 7. _____ and money to 8. _____ the 9. _____ and land use of food producers and to ensure that they have fewer problems when they buy and 10. _____ their products.

S: That sounds great.

SELF-ASSESSMENT on CEFR-J CAN-DO Descriptor

Turn to page 7 and determine which CAN-DO Descriptor(s) you have achieved.

SDG 3: Good Health and Well-Being

INTRODUCTION

1. What do you think the third SDG of Good Health and Well-Being is about?
2. Draw a different image to represent this SDG. Explain your image and compare it to the UN's official image.

VOCABULARY CD 1 - 13 ▶ 13

Listen to the essential words to SDGs and their definitions, and fill in each blank with the words you hear.

1. Provide (v): To _____
2. Childbirth (n): The _____ of having a _____
3. Childhood (n): The time of _____ between being a _____ and a _____
4. Targets (n): Things that you _____ at, or _____
5. Epidemics (n): A _____ which has _____ to many people
6. Traffic (n): Cars, trucks, _____ etc. on a road
7. Accident (n): Something done without someone _____ to do it

Fill in the blanks with the correct words below.

A. There was an _____ when somebody slipped on a wet floor.
B. In poor countries, many people get sick from malaria and tuberculosis _____.
C. Two _____ for me this year are to lose five kilograms and get my license.
D. I am sorry that I am late. There was a lot of _____ on the highway.
E. Our boss is going to _____ the drinks and the meat for the barbeque.
F. _____ is very painful for women.
G. In my _____, I learned how to ride a bicycle.

provide   childbirth   childhood   targets   epidemics   traffic   accident

READING

Q1. What do you think you will read about in terms of health?

Q2. Do you think health is a big problem in the world right now?

Q3. What do you think the UN plans to do about health?

SDG 3: Good Health and Well-Being

CD 1 - 14 ▶ 14

The third SDG is "Good Health and Well-Being." Good health and well-being mean that people feel well. Working to **provide** good health and well-being helps people live longer. It also helps more mothers to survive **childbirth** and their babies to make it through **childhood** alive. Although there has been growing success in the past in these areas, more work is needed to end diseases that cause
5   health problems. Millions can be saved through better health systems and cleaner environments.

The UN has many plans for the third SDG. First, the UN has the following **targets** for the health of mothers and children. By 2030, it wants to limit the number of mothers who die in childbirth to 70 per 100, 000 births, reduce the number of newborn child deaths to 12 per 1,000, and lower the number of children who die before the age of five to 25 per 1,000. Second, by 2030, the UN aims
10 at ending **epidemics** of several diseases, including AIDS, malaria, and tuberculosis. Moreover, it wants to reduce the number of deaths from pollution and drug abuse, and it hopes for a 50% drop in **traffic accident** deaths. Third, the UN plans to improve health care systems (especially in developing countries) by ensuring access to care and affordable medicines and vaccines for everyone.

Words and Phrases

Read each definition and find the equivalent word used in the Passage above.

1.	N _ _ _ _ _ _	Recently or just born
2.	L _ _ _ _	To restrict or reduce
3.	T _ _ _ _ _ _ _ _ _ _ _	A serious infectious disease that affects especially your lungs
4.	M _ _ _ _ _ _	A disease that you get when some types of mosquitoes bite you, which causes you fever and shivering
5.	E _ _ _ _ _ _ _	Guaranteeing
6.	A _ _ _ _	The improper use of something
7.	A _ _ _ _ _ _ _ _ _	Inexpensive; reasonably priced
8.	V _ _ _ _ _ _ s	Something used as a medicine to protect you from diseases
9.	M _ _ _ _ _ _ _	Also; furthermore; in addition
10.	D _ _ _ _ _ _ s	Illnesses; disorders of mind or body

Main Idea Q. What is this SDG focused on?

    a. Limiting how many mothers give birth

    b. Educating people about physical fitness

    c. Reducing sickness and death

    d. Both a and c

Details 1. How many people can be saved through improved health systems and cleaner environments?

_____

2. By 2030, what is the UN's goal for children under five years old?

_____

3. What three epidemics does the UN plan to end by 2030?

_____

4. What are three other causes of death that are mentioned aside from disease?

_____

5. Where does the UN especially want to improve health care systems?

_____

EXPRESS YOUR OPINION

If you could immediately end only one of the epidemics in the reading (i.e., AIDS, malaria, or tuberculosis), which one would you end?

1. *Write your opinion and its reason concisely.*

```



```

2. *Explain your opinion and its reason concisely to your classmates.*

SDG 3: Good Health and Well-Being **21**

LISTENING: Sakura's Questions About SDG 3: Good Health and Well-Being

What is Sakura going to ask her professor about SDG 3?

Listening Comprehension Questions

Prediction: *Listen to the dialogue and circle T (True) or F (False).*

1. [T / F] "Fire away" means ask any question that you want.
2. [T / F] There has been an increase in the number of newborn deaths.
3. [T / F] The health of mothers and babies is important, but fighting disease is not.
4. [T / F] The UN is only interested in ending the AIDs epidemic.
5. [T / F] The UN wants to reduce the number of deaths from traffic accidents, drug abuse, and pollution.

Confirmation: *Try to answer the following questions and listen to the dialogue again.*

1. What was the death rate for newborns in the year 2000?
   a. 12 in a thousand   **b.** 17 in a thousand   **c.** 13 in a thousand   **d.** 30 in a thousand

2. Which one of these is a disease that the UN plans to fight?
   a. Cholera   **b.** Malaria   **c.** Hysteria   **d.** Bavaria

3. Why does the UN want to improve health care systems?
   a. To help poor people   **b.** To help everyone get treatment
   c. Both a and b   **d.** None of the above

Reflection: *Listen to the part of the dialogue and fill in the blanks.*   CD 1 - Natural 17 / Slow 18 ▶ Natural 17 / Slow 18

S=Sakura Noguchi, N=Professor Nina Jang

S: Oh, that's interesting. Well, I understand that there has been some 1._____ in improvement in this 2._____, right?

N: Yeah. In fact, the 3._____ death 4._____ for newborns 5._____ from 30 per 1,000 in 2000 down to 17 per 1,000 in 2019. By 2030, the UN wants that number to be 12 per 1,000.

S: It's good to hear that there has been 6._____, but it is 7._____ to think of even one newborn dying.

N: That's 8._____. The health of babies and their mothers is 9._____ important for sustainable development, but so is the fighting of 10._____.

SELF-ASSESSMENT on CEFR-J CAN-DO Descriptor

Turn to page 7 and determine which CAN-DO Descriptor(s) you have achieved.

SDG 4: Quality Education

INTRODUCTION

1. What do you think the fourth SDG of Quality Education is about?
2. Draw a different image to represent this SDG. Explain your image and compare it to the UN's official image.

VOCABULARY CD 1 - 19 ▶ 19

Listen to the essential words to SDGs and their definitions, and fill in each blank with the words you hear.

1. Enrollment (n): The action of being _____ officially as a _____
2. Primary (adj): The level of school for _____
3. Secondary (adj): The level of school for _____, also called _____ _____
4. Post-secondary (adj): The level of school for _____ _____, including _____ and _____
5. Vocational (adj): Education for learning a _____ or _____ _____
6. Literacy (n): The ability to _____ and _____
7. Numeracy (n): The ability to use a wide _____ of _____

Fill in the blanks with the correct words below.

A. _____ is very important if you want a career in business or science or any job where mathematics is important.
B. In _____ school, I learned how to tie my shoes for the first time.
C. I feel sorry for people who do not have _____ because I love reading and writing.
D. Because the _____ was low last semester, several teachers lost their jobs because there were not enough students to teach.
E. In my last year in _____ school, I had to decide if I wanted to go to college or university or look for a job.
F. I went to university, but my cousin went to _____ school to learn how to be a chef.
G. I had to move away from home and get my first apartment when I started _____ school because my university was not in my hometown.

enrollment   primary   secondary   post-secondary   vocational   literacy   numeracy

READING

Q1. What do you think you will read about in terms of education?

Q2. Do you think education is a big problem in the world right now?

Q3. What do you think the UN plans to do about education?

SDG 4: Quality Education

CD 1 - 20 ▶ 20

The fourth SDG is "Quality Education." Being educated helps people to find their way out of poverty. A lot of progress has been made in making education more accessible and in increasing the **enrollment** rates at all levels of education, especially for females. However, in 2018, 260 million children were still not going to school. Also today, more than 50% of all young people do not meet
5 the minimum skill levels in reading and mathematics. Moreover, COVID-19 had a very negative impact on education as well by preventing 1.6 billion young people from going to school in 2020.

The UN plans to improve the quality of education by 2030. It aims to ensure that good pre-primary education and care are available to all, that everyone can get free, good education at the **primary** and **secondary** levels, and that good **post-secondary vocational** or university education is
10 accessible and affordable. Importantly, the UN wants all levels of education to be equally available to men, women, and vulnerable individuals such as indigenous or disabled people. By 2030, the UN wants to ensure that all young people have **literacy** and **numeracy**. It also wishes to help people learn the skills and knowledge that can help them get jobs and that encourage sustainable development in terms of human rights, gender equality, and non-violence. To meet these goals, the UN hopes
15 to increase the number of good schools, scholarships, and qualified teachers that are available for learners in developing countries.

Words and Phrases

Read each definition and find the equivalent word used in the Passage above.

1.	S _ _ _ _ _ _ _ _ _ s	Amounts of money given to excellent students to help pay for their education
2.	D _ _ _ _ _ _ _	Unable to use a part of the body or to learn easily
3.	A _ _ _ _ _ _ _ _	Able to use or obtain
4.	N _ _ - _ _ _ _ _ _ _ _	The policy of using peaceful methods rather than force
5.	Q _ _ _ _ _ _ _ _	Having suitable knowledge, experience, or skills for a particular job
6.	F _ _ _ _ _	Being a woman or girl, not a man or boy
7.	P _ _ _ _ _ _ _	A movement forward toward a goal
8.	M _ _ _ _ _ _ _ _ _ _	The science of numbers, quantities, shapes, and space, also math
9.	A _ _ _ _ _ _ _ _ _	Easy to get to, reach, enter, etc.
10.	I _ _ _ _ _ _ _ _	Native

Main Idea **Q.** What does the UN primarily hope to do in terms of SDG 4?

      a. To make education accessible to more people

      b. To prevent 1.6 billion young people from going to school

      c. To improve the quality of education

      d. Both a and c

Details **1.** How many children were not going to school in 2018?

_____

2. What percentage of children have numeracy and literacy problems today?

_____

3. What levels of education does SDG 4 target?

_____

4. What are two examples of sustainable development that the UN hopes to encourage through education?

_____

5. What three things does the UN want to increase to achieve SDG 4?

_____

EXPRESS YOUR OPINION

If you were not going to school, how could you become literate and numerate?

1. *Write your opinion and its reason concisely.*

2. *Explain your opinion and its reason concisely to your classmates.*

LISTENING: Sakura's Questions About SDG 4: Quality Education

What is Sakura going to ask her professor about SDG 4?

Listening Comprehension Questions

1st Listening

Prediction: *Listen to the dialogue and circle T (True) or F (False).*

1. [T / F] Professor Swain is happy about the improvements in education over the last decade.
2. [T / F] The UN mainly focuses on improving the education of boys.
3. [T / F] The UN is interested in improving only two levels of education.
4. [T / F] The UN wants to improve educational resources.
5. [T / F] Educational resources include water, gold, and oil.

2nd Listening

Confirmation: *Try to answer the following questions and listen to the dialogue again.*

1. What enrollment rates are up?
   a. Only the rates for girls
   b. The rates at all levels
   c. Only the rates for disabled and indigenous people
   d. None of them

2. What levels of education are mentioned?
   a. Pre-primary and post-secondary
   b. Primary and secondary
   c. High school and university
   d. Both a and b

3. Which education resources were mentioned?
   a. Scholarships
   b. New schools
   c. Teachers
   d. All of the above

3rd Listening

Reflection: *Listen to the part of the dialogue and fill in the blanks.*

S=Sakura Noguchi, A=Professor Alister Swain

A: Indeed, it is. As an educator, I know the difference a quality education can make, and I have been quite 1. _____ to see the improvement in this area over the past 2. _____. Enrollment rates are up at all 3. _____, and more girls than ever are getting the education they 4. _____.

S: I noticed that the UN is really focusing on ensuring that girls get 5. _____ 6. _____ to quality education.

A: Yes, and other vulnerable groups, as well, such as indigenous and 7. _____ people.

S: 8. _____. It sounds as if things are going well.

A: Yes, but with 50% of young people still doing very poorly in 9. _____ and 10. _____, much still needs to improve.

SELF-ASSESSMENT on CEFR-J CAN-DO Descriptor

Turn to page 7 and determine which CAN-DO Descriptor(s) you have achieved.

SDG 5: Gender Equality

INTRODUCTION

1. What do you think the fifth SDG of Gender Equality is about?
2. Draw a different image to represent this SDG. Explain your image and compare it to the UN's official image.

VOCABULARY `CD` 1 - 25 ▶ 25

Listen to the essential words to SDGs and their definitions, and fill in each blank with the words you hear.

1. Gender (n): The actions and _____ that make some people _____ and others _____
2. Privileges (n): _____ or _____ that some people have and others do not
3. Suffered (v): To have experienced _____ or _____
4. Genital (adj): Referring to human _____ _____
5. Mutilation (n): _____ of something
6. Discrimination (n): Bad _____ of a group of people because they are members of one _____ rather than another
7. Inheritance (n): Something that is _____ which is given to you by people after they die

Fill in the blanks with the correct words below.

A. In some countries, women are not allowed to drive because they are female. This kind of _____ makes life difficult for them.
B. Sexually transmitted diseases often cause problems in the _____ area.
C. When my grandparents died, they left me some money. I used that _____ to pay for university.
D. War results in a lot of physical _____. Soldiers sometimes lose legs or arms or get terrible injuries from bombs or bullets.
E. The Ukrainian people _____ a lot because of the Russian invasion of their country.
F. People in wealthy countries have many _____ that citizens of poor countries do not have, such as good roads, clean drinking water, and excellent hospitals.
G. _____ equality means that males and females are treated equally.

gender   privileges   suffered   genital   mutilation   discrimination   inheritance

READING

Q1. What do you think you will read about in terms of gender equality in the reading?

Q2. Do you think gender equality is a big problem in the world right now?

Q3. What do you think the UN plans to do about gender equality?

SDG 5: Gender Equality

CD 1 - 26 ▶ 26

The fifth SDG is "**Gender** Equality." Gender equality is when men and women are treated in the same way and have the same rights and **privileges**. There has been improvement in gender equality in the past few decades. More girls are being educated, and fewer are being forced into marriage at a young age. Also, more women are getting leadership positions, and more laws are being changed to

5 support equality between the sexes. However, in many places there are still social beliefs and laws that treat women as less than equal to men. Moreover, there are many more male leaders than there are female ones. Also, the amount of physical and sexual violence **suffered** by women is a big problem, with 1 in 5 women reporting such abuse within a 12-month period.

There are several ways to reach the fifth SDG. One way is by protecting the health of women.

10 For example, the UN wants to end violence against women, including ending female **genital mutilation**. Also, the UN is going to improve women's lives by giving them equal access to political and economic leadership positions. Furthermore, it hopes to recognize and value unpaid care and domestic work, and to promote shared responsibility between the sexes for that labour. Finally, the UN is going to push for the end of **discrimination** against women by promoting gender equality and

15 the empowerment of women. It wants women to have equal access to economic resources, including property ownership, financial services, **inheritance**, and natural resources.

Words and Phrases

Read each definition and find the equivalent word used in the Passage above.

1.	S _ _ _ _ _	Possessed in common with others
2.	L _ _ _ _ _ _ _ _ _	Being a leader
3.	P _ _ _ _ _ _ _	A thing or things owned by someone; possessions
4.	D _ _ _ _ _	A period of ten years
5.	O _ _ _ _ _ _ _ _	The right of owning or possessing something
6.	E _ _ _ _ _ _ _ _ _ _	Giving someone the authority or power to do something
7.	R _ _ _ _ _ _ _ _ _ _ _ _ _	A duty to deal with or take care of someone or something
8.	M _ _ _ _ _ _ _	The formal union of two partners
9.	P _ _ _ _ _ _	To support or encourage something
10.	R _ _ _ _ _ _ _ _	To become aware of or to notice

Main Idea   Q. What is the main idea of the reading?

        a. Gender equality has improved recently.

        b. Men and women should be treated differently.

        c. Changes are needed for men and women to be treated equally.

        d. Men and women have always been treated the same.

Details   1. What has happened over the past few decades in relation to gender equality?

_____

2. What indicates that violence against women is a big problem?

_____

3. What is one way that the UN wants to end violence against women?

_____

4. What kind of positions does the UN want women to have equal access to?

_____

5. What are four types of economic resources that the UN wants women to have equal access to?

_____

EXPRESS YOUR OPINION

If you were the leader of your country, how could you promote the empowerment of women?

1. *Write your opinion and its reason concisely.*

2. *Explain your opinion and its reason concisely to your classmates.*

LISTENING: Sakura's Questions About SDG 5: Gender Equality

CD 1 - Natural 27 / Slow 28   ▶   Natural 27 / Slow 28

What is Sakura going to ask her professor about SDG 5?

Listening Comprehension Questions

1st Listening

 Prediction: *Listen to the dialogue and circle T (True) or F (False).*

1. [T / F] Professor Jang and Sakura feel the same way about gender equality.
2. [T / F] Things are becoming worse for women.
3. [T / F] Violence against women is the most serious gender-related problem.
4. [T / F] Professor Jang is not surprised about genital mutilation.
5. [T / F] The UN wants women to have more political power.

2nd Listening

 Confirmation: *Try to answer the following questions and listen to the dialogue again.*

1. What is happening to more and more females?
   a. They are getting educated.   **b.** They are taking leadership positions.
   c. Both a and b   **d.** They are being shocked.

2. How many women report abuse?
   a. None   **b.** 20%   **c.** Some in 2005   **d.** 2 in 5

3. What does the UN want women to have equal access to?
   a. Fair stances   **b.** Free courses   **c.** Inheritances   **d.** Reliable sources

3rd Listening

Reflection: *Listen to the part of the dialogue and fill in the blanks.*   CD 1 - Natural 29 / Slow 30   ▶   Natural 29 / Slow 30

S=Sakura Noguchi, N=Professor Nina Jang

S: I was really 1. _____ to find out that the 2. _____ SDG is about

   3. _____ equality because I hate it when someone thinks I can't do something because I'm

   female.

N: I can't stand that 4. _____. Fortunately, that is happening less now than it

   5. _____ to 6. _____.

S: Yes. I 7. _____ that 8. _____ and 8. _____ females are getting

   educated and taking leadership positions. Still, I think that there is a lot of 9. _____ that

   needs to be 10. _____.

SELF-ASSESSMENT on CEFR-J CAN-DO Descriptor

Turn to page 7 and determine which CAN-DO Descriptor(s) you have achieved.

SDG 6: Clean Water and Sanitation

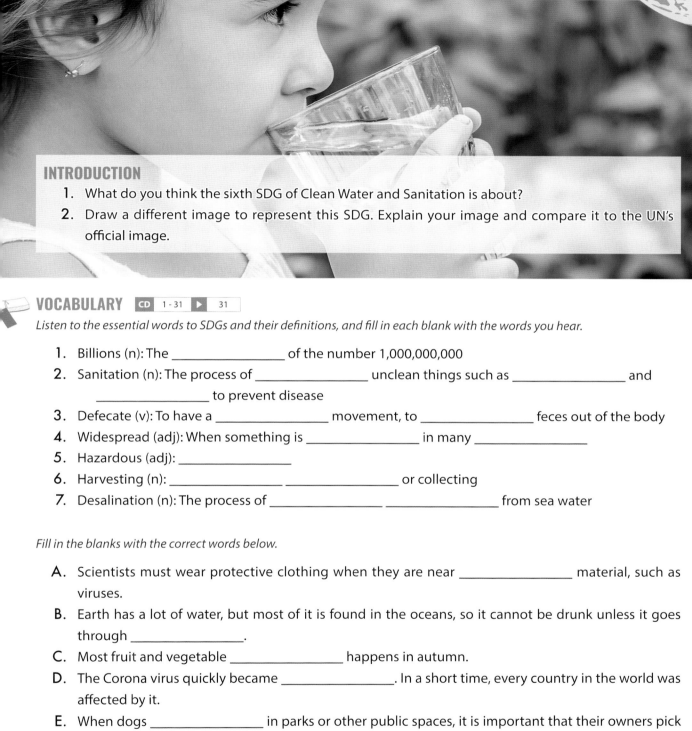

INTRODUCTION

1. What do you think the sixth SDG of Clean Water and Sanitation is about?
2. Draw a different image to represent this SDG. Explain your image and compare it to the UN's official image.

VOCABULARY   CD 1 - 31 ▶ 31

Listen to the essential words to SDGs and their definitions, and fill in each blank with the words you hear.

1. Billions (n): The _____ of the number 1,000,000,000
2. Sanitation (n): The process of _____ unclean things such as _____ and _____ to prevent disease
3. Defecate (v): To have a _____ movement, to _____ feces out of the body
4. Widespread (adj): When something is _____ in many _____
5. Hazardous (adj): _____
6. Harvesting (n): _____ _____ or collecting
7. Desalination (n): The process of _____ _____ from sea water

Fill in the blanks with the correct words below.

A. Scientists must wear protective clothing when they are near _____ material, such as viruses.
B. Earth has a lot of water, but most of it is found in the oceans, so it cannot be drunk unless it goes through _____.
C. Most fruit and vegetable _____ happens in autumn.
D. The Corona virus quickly became _____. In a short time, every country in the world was affected by it.
E. When dogs _____ in parks or other public spaces, it is important that their owners pick up the feces.
F. Wealthy countries spend a lot of money on _____ to protect people from the illnesses that can occur when sewage is not disposed of correctly.
G. Elon Musk is very rich. His companies are worth _____ of dollars.

billions   sanitation   defecate   widespread   hazardous   harvesting   desalination

READING

Q1. What do you think you will read about in terms of clean water and sanitation in the reading?

Q2. Do you think clean water and sanitation are big problems in the world right now?

Q3. What do you think the UN plans to do about clean water and sanitation?

6 CLEAN WATER AND SANITATION

SDG 6: Clean Water and Sanitation

CD 1 - 32 ▶ 32

The sixth SDG is "Clean Water and Sanitation." Many more people now have clean drinking water than in the past. However, not having clean drinking water is still a major problem for **billions** of people, especially people who do not live in cities. In fact, one out of three people still do not have clean drinking water that is easily available to them. In addition, two out of five do not have access
5 to somewhere where they can wash their hands with water and soap. Another **sanitation** problem is that more than 673 million people still **defecate** (have bowel movements) in the open rather than in toilets. Such unhealthy conditions make frequent and **widespread** illnesses far more likely.

By 2030, the UN plans to address these problems in many ways. First it wants all people to have adequate sanitation and to end open defecation. Another target is to make water quality
10 better by decreasing pollution, especially in terms of the release of **hazardous** chemicals. It also aims to increase water-use efficiency and the safe reuse of recycled water while reducing by half the proportion of untreated wastewater worldwide. Internationally, the UN hopes for international cooperation to assist developing countries improve water and sanitation projects, including water **harvesting** and **desalination**. At the domestic level, the UN will encourage greater participation
15 from local communities in improving their management of water and sanitation.

Words and Phrases

Read each definition and find the equivalent word used in the Passage above.

1.	P _ _ _ _ _ _ _ _	A part of a whole
2.	C _ _ _ _ _ _ ies	Particular areas or places considered together with the people living in them
3.	F _ _ _ _ _ _ _	Happening often; numerous
4.	D _ _ _ _ _ _ _	Of one's own country, not foreign or international
5.	C _ _ _ _ _ _ _ _ _ _	The process of working or acting together for a common purpose
6.	A _ _ _ _ _ _ _	Satisfactory or acceptable in quality or quantity; good enough in quality
7.	M _ _ _ _ _ _ _ _ _	The process of handling or controlling
8.	E _ _ _ _ _ _ _ _ _	Doing something in the best way using the fewest resources
9.	C _ _ _ _ _ _ _ s	Substances obtained by or used in chemical processes
10.	R _ _ _ _ _ _	The act of letting something go on freeing it

Main Idea Q. Which is the best summary of the first paragraph?

      a. Many people need clean drinking water and proper sanitation.

      b. Many more people now have clean drinking water.

      c. Many people need access to water and soap to wash their hands.

      d. Many people are ill because they don't have clean drinking water.

Details 1. How many people still have the major problem of not having clean drinking water?

_____

2. What problem do two out of five people have?

_____

3. Why is defecating in the open a problem?

_____

4. How can the UN improve water quality?

_____

5. What does the UN need international cooperation for?

_____

EXPRESS YOUR OPINION

If you were alone on an uninhabited island, how could you get clean drinking water?

1. *Write your opinion and its reason concisely.*

```



```

2. *Explain your opinion and its reason concisely to your classmates.*

LISTENING: Sakura's Questions About SDG 6: Clean Water and Sanitation

CD 1 - Natural 33 / Slow 34 ▶ Natural 33 / Slow 34

Listening Comprehension Questions

> What is Sakura going to ask her professor about SDG 6?

1st Listening

Prediction: *Listen to the dialogue and circle T (True) or F (False).*

1. [T / F] Sakura has always known how lucky she is to be able to drink clean drinking water anytime.
2. [T / F] Professor Swain thinks it's wonderful that billions of people around the world are privileged.
3. [T / F] Sakura is surprised that so many people can't wash their hands before they eat or make meals.
4. [T / F] Professor Swain is not surprised about how many illnesses there are in the developing world.
5. [T / F] Sakura believes that the UN's plans won't make a big difference.

2nd Listening

Confirmation: *Try to answer the following questions and listen to the dialogue again.*

1. How many people don't have access to clean drinking water?
   a. Millions   b. Trillions   c. Zillions   d. Billions

2. What is true about illnesses?
   a. Sakura is not surprised they are widespread in the developing world.
   b. Professor Swain is surprised they are widespread in the developing world.
   c. Professor Swain is not surprised they are widespread in the developing world.
   d. Professor Swain is not surprised they are widespread in the developed world.

3. How does the UN plan to improve the quality of water around the world?
   a. By decreasing the dilution of water by using hazardous chemicals
   b. By increasing solutions that use hazardous chemicals
   c. By decreasing pollution caused by hazardous chemicals
   d. None of the above

3rd Listening

Reflection: *Listen to the part of the dialogue and fill in the blanks.*   CD 1 - Natural 35 / Slow 36 ▶ Natural 35 / Slow 36
S=Sakura Noguchi, A=Professor Alister Swain

A: It ₁._____ is something, Sakura. Isn't it ₂._____ that ₃._____ of people around the world don't have that privilege?

S: It ₄._____ is. Also, it is ₅._____ that 40 percent of the people around the world don't have easy access to a place where they can wash their ₆._____ with soap and water before ₇._____ or eating food. I can't believe that.

A: Right, and when you ₈._____ that with 673 million people defecating out in the open, it comes as no ₉._____ that illnesses are so ₁₀._____ in developing countries.

SELF-ASSESSMENT on CEFR-J CAN-DO Descriptor

Turn to page 7 and determine which CAN-DO Descriptor(s) you have achieved.

SDG 7: Affordable and Clean Energy

INTRODUCTION

1. What do you think the seventh SDG of Affordable and Clean Energy is about?
2. Draw a different image to represent this SDG. Explain your image and compare it to the UN's official image.

VOCABULARY CD 1-37 ▶ 37

Listen to the essential words to SDGs and their definitions, and fill in each blank with the words you hear.

1. Efficiency (n): Doing something in the best way using the _____ _____
2. Humanity (n): _____
3. Dirty (adj): _____
4. Emissions (n): The _____ of something such as a _____ that happens as a _____ of a process such as using a car _____
5. Renewable (adj): Something like the _____ from the _____ or wind that is almost _____, such that it can be used again and again as a _____
6. Fossil fuel (n): A power source like _____ or _____ that comes from the _____ _____ of ancient plants and animals
7. Infrastructure (n): The basic systems and services that a society _____ _____ to survive such as roads, sewage systems, and _____ _____

Fill in the blanks with the correct words below.

A. _____ sources of energy include solar and wind power.
B. Japanese cars turn off at red lights to reduce _____.
C. Invading armies usually destroy power plants, bridges, and other forms of _____ to make life difficult for the society they are attacking.
D. _____ comes from the carbon that was left from dinosaurs and other ancient life forms.
E. Don't eat that. It fell on the ground, and now it is _____.
F. As far as we know, _____ is the only form of intelligent life in the universe.
G. Japanese cars are famous for fuel _____. They can drive for a long time using very little fuel.

efficiency   humanity   dirty   emissions   renewable   fossil fuel   infrastructure

READING

Q1. What do you think you will read about in terms of affordable and clean energy in the reading?

Q2. Do you think affordable and clean energy are big problems in the world right now?

Q3. What do you think the UN plans to do about affordable and clean energy?

SDG 7: Affordable and Clean Energy

CD 1 - 38 ▶ 38

The seventh SDG is "Affordable and Clean Energy." There are three fundamental issues that SDG 7 is concerned with: 1) access to energy, 2) energy **efficiency**, and 3) **renewable** energy. Like many SDGs, progress has been made in these areas, but more needs to be done. Modern electricity is still not accessible for 9.56% of **humanity**, and 2.4 billion people still heat their homes and cook

5 their food using unclean sources of fuel, including wood, coal, and even animal feces. Burning such **dirty** fuels for energy causes indoor air pollution which resulted in 3.2 million deaths in 2020. Finally, despite an increase in the use of renewable power sources, energy use contributes to 60% of global greenhouse gas **emissions**.

The UN has set targets to address the problem of affordable and clean energy. By 2030, it aims

10 to make affordable, reliable, and modern energy available to everyone. Also, it will greatly increase the amount of renewable energy used globally. It hopes to double energy efficiency around the world. This will require improving international cooperation to develop renewable energy as well as cleaner **fossil fuel** technology. The UN will focus especially on improving the energy **infrastructure** of developing countries.

Words and Phrases

Read each definition and find the equivalent word used in the Passage above.

1.	R _ _ _ _ _ _ _	Something or someone that can be trusted
2.	E _ _ _ _ _ _ _ _ _ _	A form of energy usually supplied as electric current for heating, lighting, etc.
3.	F _ _ _ _ _ _ _ _ _ _	Primary; very important
4.	C _ _ _	A hard, black mineral which burns and supplies heat
5.	C _ _ _ _ _ _ _ _ _ s	To be one of the causes of something
6.	C _ _ _ _ _ _ _ _	To be connected with; to be related to
7.	A _ _ _ _ _ _	To think about and begin to deal with
8.	R _ _ _ _ _ _	To need for a particular purpose
9.	F _ _ _	Material such as coal, gas, or oil that can be burned to produce heat or power
10.	D _ _ _ _ _ _	In spite of

Main Idea Q. What is the main idea of the first paragraph?

      a. To explain why indoor air pollution kills so many people

      b. To describe the problems caused by cleaner fossil fuel technology

      c. To demonstrate what is wrong with a lack of clean and affordable energy

      d. To demonstrate that the problem of the lack of clean and affordable energy will be solved by 2030

Details 1. What percentage of people do not have access to modern electricity?

    _____

    2. How many people still use unclean fuels to heat their homes and cook their food?

    _____

    3. What causes indoor air pollution?

    _____

    4. What does the UN plan to do in terms of global energy efficiency?

    _____

    5. Does the UN intend to end the use of fossil fuels? Explain.

    _____

EXPRESS YOUR OPINION

If you did not have access to modern electricity, how could you survive for one week?

1. *Write your opinion and its reason concisely.*

2. *Explain your opinion and its reason concisely to your classmates.*

LISTENING: Sakura's Questions About SDG 7: Affordable and Clean Energy

CD 1 - Natural 39 / Slow 40 ▶ Natural 39 / Slow 40

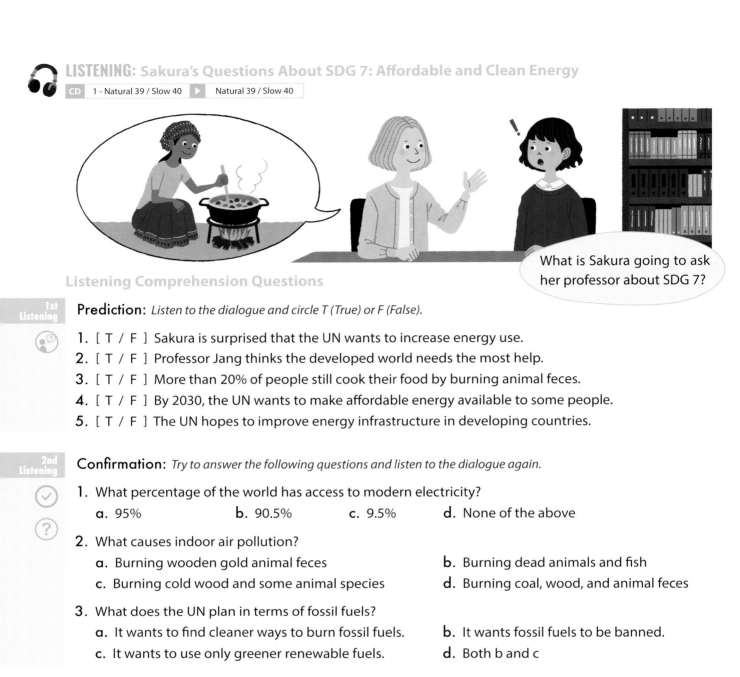

What is Sakura going to ask her professor about SDG 7?

Listening Comprehension Questions

1st Listening

Prediction: *Listen to the dialogue and circle T (True) or F (False).*

1. [T / F] Sakura is surprised that the UN wants to increase energy use.
2. [T / F] Professor Jang thinks the developed world needs the most help.
3. [T / F] More than 20% of people still cook their food by burning animal feces.
4. [T / F] By 2030, the UN wants to make affordable energy available to some people.
5. [T / F] The UN hopes to improve energy infrastructure in developing countries.

2nd Listening

Confirmation: *Try to answer the following questions and listen to the dialogue again.*

1. What percentage of the world has access to modern electricity?
   a. 95%   b. 90.5%   c. 9.5%   d. None of the above

2. What causes indoor air pollution?
   a. Burning wooden gold animal feces   b. Burning dead animals and fish
   c. Burning cold wood and some animal species   d. Burning coal, wood, and animal feces

3. What does the UN plan in terms of fossil fuels?
   a. It wants to find cleaner ways to burn fossil fuels.   b. It wants fossil fuels to be banned.
   c. It wants to use only greener renewable fuels.   d. Both b and c

3rd Listening

Reflection: *Listen to the part of the dialogue and fill in the blanks.*

CD 1 - Natural 41 / Slow 42 ▶ Natural 41 / Slow 42

S=Sakura Noguchi, N=Professor Nina Jang

N: Indeed, it is. That's why the UN is 1. _____ at making affordable, 2. _____, and 3. _____ energy 4. _____ to everyone by 2030.

S: How is it going to do that?

N: It is going to 5. _____ international 6. _____ in developing more 7. _____ energy and also in creating cleaner 8. _____ for burning fossil 9. _____.

S: What else?

N: It is going to 10. _____ on improving the energy infrastructure in developing countries.

SELF-ASSESSMENT on CEFR-J CAN-DO Descriptor

Turn to page 7 and determine which CAN-DO Descriptor(s) you have achieved.

SDG 8: Decent Work and Economic Growth

INTRODUCTION

1. What do you think the eighth SDG of Decent Work and Economic Growth is about?
2. Draw a different image to represent this SDG. Explain your image and compare it to the UN's official image.

VOCABULARY CD 1-43 ▶ 43

Listen to the essential words to SDGs and their definitions, and fill in each blank with the words you hear.

1. Decent (adj): Having a _____ _____
2. Wealth (n): Money or _____
3. Secure (adj): _____
4. Unemployment (n): The _____ of not having a _____
5. Forced (adj): Having to do something, and not being _____ to do it
6. Labour (n): _____
7. Promote (v): To _____ or _____ something

Fill in the blanks with the correct words below.

A. _____ is dangerous because without a job, you cannot buy food.
B. These advertisements _____ Coca-Cola as a delicious drink.
C. My Internet connection is _____ because I use anti-virus software.
D. Everyone should get paid for their _____. No one should be a slave.
E. _____ marriage occurs when someone must marry someone that they do not want to marry.
F. I hope this shop has _____ ramen. The ramen at the place we went to last week was not good.
G. You should try to increase your _____ when you are young, so you will not be poor when you get old.

decent   wealth   secure   unemployment   forced   labour   promote

READING

Q1. What do you think you will read about in terms of decent work and economic growth in the reading?

Q2. Do you think decent work and economic growth are big problems in the world right now?

Q3. What do you think the UN plans to do about decent work and economic growth?

SDG 8: Decent Work and Economic Growth

CD 1 - 44 ▶ 44

The eighth SDG is "**Decent** Work and Economic Growth." Economic growth means that a country's **wealth** increases as it produces more goods and services. Economic growth creates more decent jobs. Decent jobs are **secure** jobs that workers can be sure that they can keep for a long time. They are jobs that pay enough money for workers to afford food and housing. In 2017, the global
5 **unemployment** rate (the percentage of people without a job) had decreased from 6.4% in 2000 to 5.6%, but 61% of workers did not have decent jobs. Also, more men are employed than women, and they have higher paying jobs. Women do 2.6 times the unpaid care and work in the home, and women earn 23% less money than men do worldwide.

The UN has many plans to accomplish the goal of decent work and economic growth. It hopes
10 to increase economic growth, especially for poorer countries, by encouraging countries to focus on parts of their economies that create many jobs. The UN also wants to stop **forced labour** around the world. By 2025, the UN hopes to end all child labour. It is encouraging countries to reduce unemployment by increasing education and training. By 2030, it hopes to achieve full employment for everyone. It wants to develop sustainable tourism that will create jobs and **promote** local culture
15 and products. Importantly, the UN is going to encourage countries to have better labour rights, so men and women can get safe and secure jobs that pay well.

Words and Phrases

Read each definition and find the equivalent word used in the Passage above.

1.	P _ _ _ _ _ _ _ _ _	A rate in each hundred
2.	T _ _ _ _ _ _	The business activities connected with providing services such as accommodations, food etc. for travelers
3.	G _ _ _ _	Things that are produced in order to be sold
4.	I _ _ _ _ _ _ _ s	To become greater in degree, number, size, etc.
5.	A _ _ _ _ _	To have enough money to pay for something
6.	S _ _ _ _ _ _ s	Actions that benefit someone
7.	E _ _ _ _ _ ies	The wealth and resources of a country or region
8.	A _ _ _ _ _ _ _ _ _	To achieve or complete successfully
9.	H _ _ _ _ _	A place to live, such as an apartment or a house
10.	G _ _ _ _ _	An increase in economic activity

Reading Comprehension Questions

Main Idea **Q.** How are decent work and economic growth related to each other?

    a. Economic growth reduces forced labour.

    b. Economic growth occurs when a country produces more goods and services.

    c. The decrease in the unemployment rate has caused economic growth.

    d. Economic growth leads to more employment opportunities.

Details **1.** What was the unemployment rate in 2017?

_____

2. Was unemployment worse in 2000 or in 2017?

_____

3. Who gets paid less globally, men or women?

_____

4. What does the UN want to end by 2025?

_____

5. What will be the benefits of sustainable tourism?

_____

EXPRESS YOUR OPINION

If you were the mayor of a city, how could you achieve full employment for everyone?

1. *Write your opinion and its reason concisely.*

```



```

2. *Explain your opinion and its reason concisely to your classmates.*

LISTENING: Sakura's Questions About SDG 8: Decent Work and Economic Growth

CD 1 - Natural 45 / Slow 46 ▶ Natural 45 / Slow 46

Listening Comprehension Questions

> What is Sakura going to ask her professor about SDG 8?

1st Listening

Prediction: *Listen to the dialogue and circle T (True) or F (False).*

1. [T / F] At first, Sakura doesn't understand what "decent jobs" are.
2. [T / F] Being a teacher is not a decent job.
3. [T / F] Many people do casual labour.
4. [T / F] Sakura was surprised by the percentage of people who do informal labour.
5. [T / F] The UN only wants to help women get better jobs.

2nd Listening

Confirmation: *Try to answer the following questions and listen to the dialogue again.*

1. Which job is not casual labour?
   a. Migrant fruit picker
   b. Banker
   c. Temporary construction worker
   d. Underpaid factory worker

2. What percentage of work was informal in 2016?
   a. 16%
   b. 51%
   c. 61%
   d. None of the above

3. Why does the UN want to help migrant workers?
   a. They are citizens of the countries where they work.
   b. Their work is dangerous sometimes.
   c. They often get paid very little for their work.
   d. Both b and c

3rd Listening

Reflection: *Listen to the part of the dialogue and fill in the blanks.*

CD 1 - Natural 47 / Slow 48 ▶ Natural 47 / Slow 48

S=Sakura Noguchi, A=Professor Alister Swain

S: So then, what kinds of jobs are not ₁. _____?

A: These are jobs where the worker is just a helper, and only works ₂. _____ they ₃. _____ a job, like a person who is ₄. _____ cash to help finish building a house or do some ₅. _____. This work is sometimes called informal or casual labour, and it ₆. _____ jobs in factories in developing countries where workers work long hours for very ₇. _____ money. Did you know that in 2016, 61% of all jobs were informal?

S: No! That's ₈. _____.

A: Yes, and that is why the UN is trying to help by encouraging countries to ₉. _____ more training and education for ₁₀. _____ and trying to reach the goal of full employment in ₁. _____ jobs for everyone by 2030.

SELF-ASSESSMENT on CEFR-J CAN-DO Descriptor

Turn to page 7 and determine which CAN-DO Descriptor(s) you have achieved.

SDG 9: Industry, Innovation, and Infrastructure

INTRODUCTION

1. What do you think the ninth SDG of Industry, Innovation, and Infrastructure is about?
2. Draw a different image to represent this SDG. Explain your image and compare it to the UN's official image.

VOCABULARY   CD 1 - 49   ▶   49

Listen to the essential words to SDGs and their definitions, and fill in each blank with the words you hear.

1. Industry (n): A group of _____ that provides a _____ or service
2. Innovation (n): Something new, or a new _____ of doing something
3. Potential (n): Having the _____ of becoming something
4. Textiles (n): Materials like _____ that are made by _____ _____ together
5. Significantly (adv): Done a lot, or in a _____ _____
6. Reliable (adj): Something or someone that can be _____
7. Technical (adj): _____ _____ about something

Fill in the blanks with the correct words below.

A. She is a very skilled dancer. She has the _____ to be a professional dancer in the future.
B. Honda makes _____ cars. You can trust that they will continue to work well for many years.
C. That factory makes _____ that are used for making clothing.
D. The price of gasoline has increased _____ from one dollar to five dollars.
E. The personal computer was the most important _____ of the 20th century.
F. Car mechanics need to learn a lot of _____ knowledge to be able to fix cars.
G. The Japanese auto _____ is known all over the world because companies like Honda and Toyota make excellent cars.

industry   innovation   potential   textiles   significantly   reliable   technical

READING

Q1. What do you think you will read about in terms of industry, innovation, and infrastructure in the reading?

Q2. Do you think industry, innovation, and infrastructure are big problems in the world right now?

Q3. What do you think the UN plans to do about industry, innovation, and infrastructure?

SDG 9: Industry, Innovation, and Infrastructure

CD 1 - 50 ▶ 50

The ninth SDG is "**Industry**, **Innovation**, and Infrastructure." An industry is a group of companies that makes something or offers a service. Innovations are new ways of doing something. Infrastructure refers to the basic systems and services that a society needs to survive such as transportation, sewage, power, communication, and financial systems. Improvement in these three
5 things makes life better economically and socially. The least developed countries have a great **potential** to improve by increasing industries that create food, clothing, and **textiles**. These countries also need to invest more in renewable energy, such as solar and wind power. In 2019, developing countries only invested 130 billion dollars, while developed countries invested 150 billion dollars. Finally, the least developed countries need to improve their communication systems because only
10 19% of their people have access to the Internet.

The UN aims to improve industry, innovation, and infrastructure. It wants countries, especially the least developed countries, to **significantly** increase their amount of industrialization by 2030. The UN will make it easier for small industrial projects in developing countries to get money. It is also going to develop **reliable** infrastructure to support economic development and a better quality
15 of life. The UN will provide financial, technological, and **technical** support to the least developed countries, including African countries and small island developing states. In addition, the UN wants universal and affordable access to the Internet in the least developed countries.

Words and Phrases

Read each definition and find the equivalent word used in the Passage above.

1.	I _ _ _ _ _ _ _ _ _ _ _ _ _ _ _	The process of developing industries in a country or region on a wide scale
2.	T _ _ _ _ _ _ _ _ _ _ _ _	A system or method of carrying passengers or goods from one place to another
3.	A _ _ _ _ _	The opportunity to use
4.	S _ _ _ _ _	The mixture of waste from human body and used water that is conveyed from houses or factories through special pipes
5.	S _ _ _ _	Of or connected with the sun
6.	B _ _ _ _ _ _	The number 1,000,000,000
7.	U _ _ _ _ _ _ _ _	Affecting all people in the world
8.	P _ _ _ _ _ _ s	Plans or schemes

9. I _ _ _ _ _   To use money in such a way as to get a profit

10. S _ _ _ _ _ _ _   In a way that relates to human society and its organization

Reading Comprehension Questions

Main Idea Q. Why is the UN worried about the least developed countries?

    a. They have not met their potential in terms of industrialization.
    b. They need to invest more money into renewable energy.
    c. They have to improve their communication systems.
    d. All of the above

Details 1. What is an example of infrastructure?

_____

2. What industries have the potential for development in the least developed countries?

_____

3. What are two examples of renewable energy?

_____

4. What do the least developed countries need to develop before 2030?

_____

5. Where is the UN going to provide technical support?

_____

EXPRESS YOUR OPINION

If you did not have affordable access to the Internet, how could you survive for one week?

1. *Write your opinion and its reason concisely.*

┌───┐
│   │
│   │
│   │
│   │
│   │
│   │
└───┘

2. *Explain your opinion and its reason concisely to your classmates.*

LISTENING: Sakura's Questions About SDG 9: Industry, Innovation, and Infrastructure

CD 1 - Natural 51 / Slow 52 ▶ Natural 51 / Slow 52

Listening Comprehension Questions

What is Sakura going to ask her professor about SDG 9?

1st Listening

Prediction: *Listen to the dialogue and circle T (True) or F (False).*

1. [T / F] Sakura was a little surprised by this SDG.
2. [T / F] The UN believes that industrialization is a good thing.
3. [T / F] The UN hopes that the least developed countries will increase industrialization more slowly.
4. [T / F] The UN does not care about the effect of industrialization on the environment.
5. [T / F] Sakura imagines that life would be better without the Internet.

2nd Listening

Confirmation: *Try to answer the following questions and listen to the dialogue again.*

1. Which statement is true?
   a. Developing countries spent 20 million dollars more on renewables than developed countries in 2019.
   b. Developing countries spent 20 million dollars less on renewables than developed countries in 2019.
   c. Developing countries spent 20 billion dollars more on renewables than developed countries in 2019.
   d. Developing countries spent 20 billion dollars less on renewables than developed countries in 2019.

2. Which word means the same as "gap"?
   a. Difference   b. Surprise   c. Mistake   d. Hat

3. Which statement is true in the least developed countries?
   a. Over 90% of people have Internet access.
   b. Only 19% of people are interested in the Internet.
   c. Only 19% of people have Internet access.
   d. Over 19% of people have Internet access.

3rd Listening

Reflection: *Listen to the part of the dialogue and fill in the blanks.*   CD 1 - Natural 53 / Slow 54 ▶ Natural 53 / Slow 54

S=Sakura Noguchi, N=Professor Nina Jang

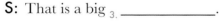

N: Yeah. In 2019 alone, 1. _____ countries invested 20 2. _____ dollars more than developing countries did into renewables.

S: That is a big 3. _____.

N: The UN is also 4. _____ that the 5. _____ 1. _____ countries are falling 6. _____ where communication and access to information are concerned.

S: I know. I couldn't believe it when I 7. _____ that only 19% of people in those countries had Internet access. 8. _____, I can't 9. _____ what I would do 10. _____ the Internet.

N: Me neither. It is one of the biggest innovations in my lifetime.

S: It definitely makes sense that the UN wants universal access to it by 2030.

SELF-ASSESSMENT on CEFR-J CAN-DO Descriptor

Turn to page 7 and determine which CAN-DO Descriptor(s) you have achieved.

SDG 10: Reduced Inequalities

INTRODUCTION

1. What do you think the tenth SDG of Reduced Inequalities is about?
2. Draw a different image to represent this SDG. Explain your image and compare it to the UN's official image.

VOCABULARY CD 2-01 ▶ 55

Listen to the essential words to SDGs and their definitions, and fill in each blank with the words you hear.

1. Disabilities (n): A _____ with your _____, such as not being able to _____ or _____
2. Rural (adj): Related to the _____
3. Urban (adj): Related to _____
4. Sexual orientation (n): Whether you are attracted to your _____ _____ or the _____ _____
5. Trade (n): The _____ of products and services
6. Institutions (n): _____ that _____ in something; a _____ is a _____ institution
7. Status (n): Your _____ _____ _____ others

Fill in the blanks with the correct words below.

A. Universities are sometimes called educational _____ because they are organizations that specialize in education.
B. In Canada, _____ is not very important. Men can marry men, and women can marry women if that is what they want to do.
C. A president has a higher _____ in a company than a vice president.
D. Fukuoka, Osaka, and Tokyo are all _____ areas.
E. It is good that many places have parking spots close to their entrances for people with _____.
F. I love to travel to _____ areas, so I can see the beauty of the countryside.
G. Rules are needed for international _____ to ensure that countries do business fairly with each other.

disabilities   rural   urban   sexual orientation   trade   institutions   status

READING

Q1. What do you think you will read about in terms of reduced inequalities in the reading?

Q2. Do you think it is important to reduce inequalities in the world right now?

Q3. How do you think the UN plans to reduce inequalities?

SDG 10: Reduced Inequalities

CD 2-02 ▶ 56

The tenth SDG is "Reduced Inequalities." An inequality occurs when some enjoy better circumstances than others. The UN wants to reduce inequalities among and within countries. Developed countries have more wealth and power than developing countries. They have better health care systems, so their people are healthier. Globally, there are 1 billion people with **disabilities**, and
5 80% of them live in developing countries. There are also inequalities within countries. In developing countries, the poorest 20% of people are three times more likely to die before the age of 5 than the richest people. Also, **rural** women are three times more likely to die while having a baby than **urban** women. There are inequalities in developed countries as well. Some people are treated worse because of their race, religion, sex, income, age, or **sexual orientation**.

10 The UN hopes to reduce inequalities in many ways. It will encourage developed countries to provide money to the developing countries that need it most. The UN also wants special treatment for developing countries in international **trade** so that they can get better trade deals. Furthermore, the UN wants more people from developing countries to have positions of power in global financial **institutions**, so they will be able to be a part of important decisions that affect them. By 2030, the
15 UN wants to significantly raise the incomes of the poorest 40% of people. It also aims to promote the social, economic, and political inclusion of all, regardless of age, sex, disability, race, religion, or economic **status**.

Words and Phrases

Read each definition and find the equivalent word used in the Passage above.

1.	S _ _ _ _ _ _ _ _ _ _ _ _	Done a lot, or in a great amount
2.	R _ _ _ _ _ _ _ _	Without concern for or without paying attention to
3.	R _ _ _	One of the major divisions of humankind based on particular physical characteristics
4.	O _ _ _ _ s	To happen or take place
5.	A _ _ _ _ _	To have an effect on or make a difference to
6.	I _ _ _ _ _ _ _ _	The action or state of being included with
7.	R _ _ _ _ _ _ _	The belief in or worship of a God or gods
8.	C _ _ _ _ _ _ _ _ _ _ s	Conditions relevant to an event or action
9.	I _ _ _ _ _ _ _ ies	Absence or lack of equalities
10.	T _ _ _ _ _ _ _	A way of dealing with a subject

Main Idea Q. What inequalities does the UN want to reduce?

    a. The inequalities for the poorest 20% of people

    b. The inequalities for the poorest 40% of people

    c. The inequalities inside and between countries

    d. The inequalities among countries

Details 1. What percentage of disabled people live in developing countries?

_____

2. In developing countries, how much more likely are poor people to die before the age of 5 than rich people?

_____

3. What is the inequality between rural and urban women in developing countries?

_____

4. Are there inequalities in developed countries? Explain.

_____

5. What does the UN want to do by 2030?

_____

EXPRESS YOUR OPINION

If you were the mayor of a city in a developing country, how could you reduce inequalities?

1. *Write your opinion and its reason concisely.*

2. *Explain your opinion and its reason concisely to your classmates.*

LISTENING: Sakura's Questions About SDG 10: Reduced Inequalities

CD 2 - Natural 03 / Slow 04 ▶ Natural 57 / Slow 58

Listening Comprehension Questions

> What is Sakura going to ask her professor about SDG 10?

1st Listening

Prediction: *Listen to the dialogue and circle T (True) or F (False).*

1. [T / F] Professor Swain thinks that inequalities among countries are more important than inequalities within countries.
2. [T / F] Sakura feels that inequalities among countries are more important than inequalities within countries.
3. [T / F] There are only inequalities within developing countries.
4. [T / F] Only 20% of all disabled people live in developed countries.
5. [T / F] Sakura understands Professor Swain's opinion.

2nd Listening

Confirmation: *Try to answer the following questions and listen to the dialogue again.*

1. Which statement is true?
   a. Sakura thinks there are more inequalities among countries than within them.
   b. Professor Swain thinks there are fewer inequalities among countries than between them.
   c. Professor Swain thinks neither inequalities between countries nor within them are important.
   d. None of the above

2. Which statement is correct about people in developing countries?
   a. Three times more poor people than rich people die before 5.
   b. Five times more poor people than rich people die before 3.
   c. Three times more rural women than urban women die while having a baby.
   d. Both a and c

3. What was said about discrimination?
   a. 3 in 10 disabled people are discriminated against.
   b. 1 in 5 people is discriminated against.
   c. Sakura is unhappy about what she learned about discrimination.
   d. All of the above

3rd Listening

Reflection: *Listen to the part of the dialogue and fill in the blanks.*   CD 2 - Natural 05 / Slow 06 ▶ Natural 59 / Slow 60

S=Sakura Noguchi, A=Professor Alister Swain

S: Do you think it's more important to 1. _____ 2. _____ among countries or within them?

A: That's a good question. I think they're both important. Both kinds of 2. _____ 3. _____ people to 4. _____, so I am not 5. _____ I think one is more important than the 6. _____.

S: I see.

A: What about you?

S: Well, the inequalities between countries seem to do a 7. _____ of 8. _____. I mean it seems so 9. _____ that 80% of disabled people are found in the developing world, and the number of people who die before 5 or 10. _____ having a baby is so high there.

SELF-ASSESSMENT on CEFR-J CAN-DO Descriptor

Turn to page 7 and determine which CAN-DO Descriptor(s) you have achieved.

SDG 11: Sustainable Cities and Communities

INTRODUCTION

1. What do you think the eleventh SDG of Sustainable Cities and Communities is about?
2. Draw a different image to represent this SDG. Explain your image and compare it to the UN's official image.

VOCABULARY CD 2-07 ▶ 61

Listen to the essential words to SDGs and their definitions, and fill in each blank with the words you hear.

1. Sustainable (adj): Something can _____ to work _____ for a
   _____ _____

2. Breaking down (v): Stop _____ _____

3. Expansion (n): To become _____

4. Slums (n): _____ where many poor people live which are in _____
   _____ and are _____

5. Managing (v): _____ or _____ how something works

6. Maintaining (v): Keeping something in _____ _____

7. Elderly (adj): _____

Fill in the blanks with the correct words below.

A. My old car kept _____, so I had to buy a new one.

B. My grandfather is 100 years old. He is an _____ man.

C. Urban _____ happens when cities grow in size.

D. It is dangerous to live in _____ because the buildings are in poor conditions, there is a lot of crime, and it is easy to get sick because of the dirty conditions.

E. My lifestyle is _____ because I make more money than I spend.

F. _____ good health requires doing regular exercise and eating healthy food.

G. He has done a good job _____ this business. Since he took charge, it has been very successful.

> sustainable   breaking down   expansion   slums   managing   maintaining   elderly

READING

Q1. What do you think you will read about in terms of sustainable cities and communities in the reading?

Q2. Do you think it is important to have sustainable cities and communities in the world right now?

Q3. How do you think the UN plans to ensure sustainable cities and communities?

SDG 11: Sustainable Cities and Communities

CD 2-08 ▶ 62

The eleventh SDG is "**Sustainable** Cities and Communities." Sustainable means that something can continue working well without **breaking down**. The UN wants all cities to not only be sustainable but also, welcoming, safe, and environmentally friendly. Now, 3.5 billion people (half the world's population) live in cities. By 2030, that number will increase to 5 billion, and by 2050, 70%
5 of humanity will live in urban areas. In the next few decades, 95% of urban **expansion** will happen in developing countries. This is a problem because 828 million people already live in **slums**. Another problem is that over 60-80% of the world's energy use and 75% of carbon emissions come from cities even though they only take up 3% of the Earth's land. Moreover, cities already have trouble getting enough fresh water, **managing** their sewage, and **maintaining** the health of their residents.

10 The UN has many things it wants to do to make cities into sustainable places for communities. By 2030, it aims to provide safe and affordable housing to all and upgrade slums. The UN also wants to provide safe, affordable transportation systems to city residents, especially for women, children, disabled and **elderly** people. This will include improved road safety and more public transportation. In addition, the UN wants to reduce the damage that cities do to the environment by paying
15 attention to air quality and waste management. Furthermore, the UN wants cities to provide safe and green public places for all the community to enjoy.

Words and Phrases

Read each definition and find the equivalent word used in the Passage above.

1. Environmentally _ _ _ _ _ _ _ _   Not harmful to the environment

2. P _ _ _ _ _   Of or concerning ordinary people in society in general

3. E _ _ _ _ _ _ _ s   The release of something such as a gas that happens as a byproduct of a process such as using a car motor

4. S _ _ _ _ _   The state of being not dangerous

5. U _ _ _ _   From the city

6. R _ _ _ _ _ _ _ s   People who live in a particular place permanently or for a long time

7. W _ _ _ _   The unusable remains or byproducts of something

8. L _ _ _   The Earth's surface that is not covered by water

9. H _ _ _ _ _ _ _   People

10. D _ _ _ _ _   Harmful effects on something or someone

Reading Comprehension Questions

Main Idea **Q.** Why is the UN worried about the sustainability of cities and communities?

a. Cities are where most people will live in the future.
b. Cities use most of our energy.
c. Cities produce the most pollution.
d. All of the above

Details **1.** How many people live in cities now?

____

2. How many people will live in cities by 2050?

____

3. Where do 828 million people live?

____

4. What is one problem caused by cities?

____

5. By 2030, what does the UN want to do?

____

EXPRESS YOUR OPINION

If you were the mayor of a city, how could you provide safe and green public places for all the communities to enjoy?

1. *Write your opinion and its reason concisely.*

2. *Explain your opinion and its reason concisely to your classmates.*

LISTENING: Sakura's Questions About SDG 11: Sustainable Cities and Communities

What is Sakura going to ask her professor about SDG 11?

Listening Comprehension Questions

 Prediction: *Listen to the dialogue and circle T (True) or F (False).*

1. [T / F] Sakura knew that 50% of people on Earth live in cities.
2. [T / F] Professor Jang is worried about the increasing number of people living in cities.
3. [T / F] Professor Jang thinks the UN plans for sustainable cities are important.
4. [T / F] Sakura supports the UN plans for sustainable cities and communities.
5. [T / F] Sakura does not care about cultural and heritage sites.

Confirmation: *Try to answer the following questions and listen to the dialogue again.*

1. Which statement is true?
   a. By 2070, 70% of humanity will live in cities.
   b. By 2030, only 30% of humanity will live in cities.
   c. By 2050, 30% of humanity will live in cities.
   d. None of the above

2. What does Professor Jang say she likes about the UN's plans?
   a. The protection of heritage sites
   b. The environmental management
   c. The public transportation
   d. Both b and c

3. What vulnerable people did Sakura mention?
   a. Elderly people   b. Disabled people   c. Children   d. Both a and c

Reflection: *Listen to the part of the dialogue and fill in the blanks.*

CD 2 - Natural 11 / Slow 12 ▶ Natural 65 / Slow 66

S=Sakura Noguchi, N=Professor Nina Jang

S: I also like their plans to 1. _____ green space for the community, especially for 2. _____ people such as women, children, and the 3. _____.

N: Oh, then you'll 4. _____ also be 5. _____ to hear that the UN is also planning to 6. _____ their efforts to protect cultural and natural 7. _____ 8. _____.

S: That is 9. _____ to hear. We have many such 8. _____ in Japan, and it's good to know that the UN supports sustainable cities that won't 10. _____ them.

SELF-ASSESSMENT on CEFR-J CAN-DO Descriptor

Turn to page 7 and determine which CAN-DO Descriptor(s) you have achieved.

SDG 12: Responsible Consumption and Production

INTRODUCTION

1. What do you think the twelfth SDG of Responsible Consumption and Production is about?
2. Draw a different image to represent this SDG. Explain your image and compare it to the UN's official image.

VOCABULARY CD 2-13 ▶ 67

Listen to the essential words to SDGs and their definitions, and fill in each blank with the words you hear.

1. Responsible (adj): Something done correctly, with _____ _____
2. Production (n): The _____ of _____ something
3. Consumption (n): The _____ of _____ something
4. Efficiently (adv): Done in the _____ way with the _____ _____
5. Rotting (v): Going bad, or becoming _____ because it was not _____
   _____ enough
6. Practices (n): _____ of doing something
7. Substantially (adv): _____

Fill in the blanks with the correct words below.

A. He uses his time at the office very _____. He never wastes time, and he always gets things done well.
B. The increase in gas _____ has made it more expensive than it used to be.
C. The bananas you bought three weeks ago are _____ now.
D. The _____ of electric cars will reduce the amount of fossil fuels that we use.
E. Banking _____ are different than they were when I was young. I used to have to go to a counter and talk to a bank worker. Now I just use the ATM.
F. Your appearance has changed _____. I remember when you had very long hair and a beard. Now, you look like a soldier.
G. _____ use of a car is very important. You must drive safely and follow all the rules of the road.

responsible production consumption efficiently rotting practices substantially

READING

Q1. What do you think you will read about in terms of responsible consumption and production in the reading?

Q2. Do you think responsible consumption and production is important in the world right now?

Q3. How do you think the UN plans to ensure responsible consumption and production?

SDG 12: Responsible Consumption and Production CD 2-14 ▶ 68

The twelfth SDG is "**Responsible Consumption** and **Production**." To consume something is to use it, and to produce something is to make it. Being responsible means acting correctly. The UN warns that humanity is not doing so because we are not using our natural resources **efficiently**, and we are damaging our environment in the way that we produce and consume things like food,
5 water, and energy. For example, each year, 1/3 of the food we produce ends up **rotting** and being thrown out by stores or customers, or it doesn't get to consumers because of poor harvesting and transportation **practices**. Furthermore, we are polluting the water in rivers and lakes faster than nature can recycle it. Also, our use of fossil fuels to produce energy damages the environment, and we do not consume that energy efficiently. For example, we could save US$120 billion every year if
10 people switched to using energy efficient lightbulbs.

The UN urges governments, companies, and individuals to produce and consume more responsibly. It wants governments to use its set of ten-year programs that will result in responsible consumption and production. The UN wants companies to reduce the waste they produce that pollutes the air, land, and water. Also, by 2030, it hopes to **substantially** reduce the amount of food
15 that is wasted due to poor practices of food production, transportation, and consumption. Moreover, by 2030, the UN wants people everywhere to be informed about how to live a sustainable lifestyle that reduces waste through prevention and recycling.

Words and Phrases

Read each definition and find the equivalent word used in the Passage above.

1.	P _ _ _ _ _ _ _ _ _	Stopping something from happening
2.	W _ _ _ s	To tell someone that something bad or dangerous may happen
3.	I _ _ _ _ _ _ _ _ _ s	People considered separately
4.	S _ _ _ _ _ ed	To change from one thing to another
5.	R _ _ _ _ _ in	To have a specified outcome
6.	R _ _ _ _ _ _ _ _	The process of treating used material or objects so that they can be used again
7.	U _ _ _ s	To advise or try hard to persuade someone to do something
8.	Energy _ _ _ _ _ _ _ _ _	Using as little energy as possible

9. A _ _ ing   To take action; to do something

10. C _ _ _ _ _ _   To buy goods or services

Main Idea   **Q.** Based on the reading, which one would be a suitable alternative title for SDG 12?

     a. Better Ways to Live
     b. Correct Utilization and Creation
     c. Reduce and Recycle
     d. Efficient Energy Use and Waste Disposal

Details   **1.** How much of the food we produce is wasted annually?

_____

2. What are two things that cause so much food to be wasted?

_____

3. How much money could be saved if everyone used environmentally friendly lightbulbs?

_____

4. Which three groups is the UN urging to produce and consume more responsibly?

_____

5. What are two ways that people can reduce waste?

_____

EXPRESS YOUR OPINION

If you were the president of an automobile manufacturing company, how could you reduce the waste it produces that pollutes the air, land, and water?

1. *Write your opinion and its reason concisely.*

```



```

2. *Explain your opinion and its reason concisely to your classmates.*

LISTENING: Sakura's Questions About SDG 12: Responsible Consumption and Production

What is Sakura going to ask her professor about SDG 12?

Listening Comprehension Questions

1st Listening

Prediction: *Listen to the dialogue and circle T (True) or F (False).*

1. [T / F] Sakura is surprised by how much money the wasted food is worth.
2. [T / F] Professor Swain explained that there is a lot of freshwater available for humans to use.
3. [T / F] Professor Swain explained that water pollution is a problem.
4. [T / F] Sakura hopes the UN can help.
5. [T / F] Professor Swain explained that if we don't change, by 2050, everything will be fine.

2nd Listening

Confirmation: *Try to answer the following questions and listen to the dialogue again.*

1. Which statement about annual food waste is not true?
   a. 1/3 of all our food is wasted.
   b. We waste 1.3 billion dollars' worth of food.
   c. We waste 1 trillion dollars' worth of food.
   d. We waste 1.3 billion tons of food.

2. What percentage of freshwater is available for humans to use?
   a. 0.5%   b. 3%   c. 2.5%   d. None of the above

3. What does Professor Swain say we will need by 2050 if we don't change?
   a. An increase in population
   b. More production and consumption
   c. To leave Earth
   d. A lot more resources

3rd Listening

Reflection: *Listen to the part of the dialogue and fill in the blanks.*
S=Sakura Noguchi, A=Professor Alister Swain

S: Did you know that every year we 1. _____ 1/3 of the food that we produce

2. _____?

A: Yes. It's 3. _____ 4. _____, isn't it? That works out to 1.3 billion 5. _____ of food, worth around one 6. _____ dollars.

S: Oh my God! That's 7. _____!

A: Here's something 8. _____ that will shock you. Under 3% of the water on Earth is drinkable, and 2.5% of that is 9. _____ in places like Antarctica, the Arctic, and 10. _____. That means humans have only 0.5% of the world's water for their freshwater needs.

SELF-ASSESSMENT on CEFR-J CAN-DO Descriptor

Turn to page 7 and determine which CAN-DO Descriptor(s) you have achieved.

SDG 13: Climate Action

INTRODUCTION

1. What do you think the thirteenth SDG of Climate Action is about?
2. Draw a different image to represent this SDG. Explain your image and compare it to the UN's official image.

VOCABULARY `CD` 2-19 ▶ 73

Listen to the essential words to SDGs and their definitions, and fill in each blank with the words you hear.

1. Climate (n): The long-term _____ of _____

2. Grain (n): A _____ from grasses like _____, corn, or _____ that is eaten by humans and animals

3. Megatons (n): _____ of _____ that are _____ to one _____ tons

4. Absorb (v): To _____ something _____, like a sponge _____ _____ water

5. Impacts (n): _____

6. Adapt (v): To _____ in _____ that are _____ and _____ you to continue when something bad happens

7. Resilient (adj): _____, able to continue _____ difficult _____

Fill in the blanks with the correct words below.

A. If you spill a drink, you can use paper towels to _____ the liquid.

B. After I broke my right arm, I had to _____ by using my left arm to do everything.

C. The _____ of earthquakes include damages to buildings and roads.

D. My 19-year-old cat, Maui, is a _____ animal. He moved from Japan to Canada. He has had many illnesses, and he has been in several fights. Yet, he is still a very energetic pet.

E. Rice is such a popular food around the world that 593 _____ of it is produced annually.

F. Hokkaido has a much cooler _____ than Kyushu.

G. Barley is a very popular type of _____ because beer can be made from it.

climate   grain   megatons   absorb   impacts   adapt   resilient

READING

Q1. What do you think you will read about in terms of climate action in the reading?
Q2. Do you think climate action is needed in the world right now?
Q3. How do you think the UN plans to pursue climate action?

SDG 13: Climate Action

CD 2 - 20 ▶ 74

The thirteenth SDG is "**Climate** Action." The climate is the pattern of weather that is measured in decades or longer. The UN warns that Earth's climate is changing. From 1880 to 2012, the global average temperature increased 0.85 degrees Celsius. For each one-degree increase, plants like wheat and corn produce 5% less **grain**. Between 1981 and 2002, grain production decreased by 40
5   **megatons** annually. The increasing temperature is causing Earth's ice to melt. From 1901 to 2010, this made the global sea level rise 19 centimeters, causing problems like flooding. The UN blames global warming on our emission of gases like carbon dioxide. These are called greenhouse gases because they **absorb** heat and prevent it from escaping, like a greenhouse traps heat from sunlight. The emissions increased more between 2000 and 2010 than in each of the three previous decades.
10 Continued emissions may cause another 1.5-degree Celsius increase by 2100.

The UN plans to fight the causes of climate change and its **impacts**. It supports the Paris Agreement's goal of limiting the global temperature increase to 1.5 degrees by 2100. This requires a 7.6% annual reduction in emissions between 2020 and 2030. The UN encourages governments to transform energy, transportation, agricultural and other systems into more environmentally friendly
15 systems. It wants governments, businesses, and individual investors to invest in climate-friendly investments, like renewable energy projects. The UN also urges developed countries to jointly raise 100 billion dollars annually to assist developing countries to **adapt** and become more **resilient** to the impacts of climate change.

Words and Phrases

Read each definition and find the equivalent word used in the Passage above.

1.	Carbon _ _ _ _ _ _ _	A colourless, odorless gas produced by burning carbon or by people and animals breathing out
2.	A _ _ _ _ _	To help someone to do something
3.	I _ _ _ _ _ _ _ s	People who use money in such a way as to get a profit
4.	M _ _ _	To become liquefied by heat
5.	F _ _ _ _	To try hard to stop or deal with something bad
6.	P _ _ _ _ _ _	The regular way in which something happens or is done
7.	A _ _ _ _ _ _ _ _ _ _ _	Having to do with the science or practice of farming
8.	A _ _ _ _ _ _ _	Once every year
9.	W _ _ _ _	A plant that makes a grain which is used to produce flour, bread, pasta, etc.
10.	T _ _ _ _ _ _ _ _	To completely change

Reading Comprehension Questions

Q. Why does the UN want to act against climate change?

    a. The Paris Agreement

    b. Climate change has many serious negative consequences.

    c. We need a 7.6% annual decrease in greenhouse gas emissions between 2020 and 2030.

    d. All of the above

Details 1. How much did the temperature increase between 1880 and 2012?

_____

2. Between 1981 and 2002, how much did grain production decrease?

_____

3. How much did the global sea level rise between 1901 and 2010?

_____

4. How many degrees does the UN want to limit the temperature increase to by the end of the century?

_____

5. To meet the Paris Agreement's goal, how much must the annual global greenhouse gas emissions be reduced?

_____

EXPRESS YOUR OPINION

If you could speak to the leaders of the countries that emit the most greenhouse gasses, how would you get them to change?

1. *Write your opinion and its reason concisely.*

```


```

2. *Explain your opinion and its reason concisely to your classmates.*

LISTENING: Sakura's Questions About SDG 13: Climate Action

CD 2 - Natural 21 / Slow 22 ▶ Natural 75 / Slow 76

> What is Sakura going to ask her professor about SDG 13?

Listening Comprehension Questions

Prediction: *Listen to the dialogue and circle T (True) or F (False).*

1. [T / F] At first, Sakura was not sure if climate change was a problem.
2. [T / F] Professor Jang said that the UN does not think climate change is a problem.
3. [T / F] The UN has the same goal as the countries that signed the Paris Agreement in terms of limiting the increase in temperature before 2100.
4. [T / F] Sakura thinks that the annual emission target is achievable.
5. [T / F] Professor Jang does not think that the pandemic had an effect on greenhouse gas emissions.

Confirmation: *Try to answer the following questions and listen to the dialogue again.*

1. How much does the UN want to limit the temperature increase by the end of the century to?
   a. 2 degrees   **b.** 7.6 degrees   **c.** A half degree   **d.** 1.5 degrees

2. Which statement is true about annual greenhouse gas emissions?
   a. They were reduced to 7.6% during the pandemic.
   b. They were reduced by more than 7.6% during the pandemic because factories were shut down.
   c. They UN wants them to be reduced by 7.6% between 2020 and 2030.
   d. They are currently reduced to 7.6%.

3. In 2016, how much money was invested in climate action?
   a. As much as was invested in fossil fuels   **b.** More than was invested in fossil fuels
   c. 781 billion dollars   **d.** Not as much as was invested in fossil fuels

Reflection: *Listen to the part of the dialogue and fill in the blanks.*

CD 2 - Natural 23 / Slow 24 ▶ Natural 77 / Slow 78

S=Sakura Noguchi, N=Professor Nina Jang

N: The UN $_1$ _____ thinks so, and they have some good $_2$ _____ for that. For example, $_3$ _____ gas emissions could cause the temperature to $_4$ _____ increase two or more $_5$ _____ Celsius before the end of the century.

S: I $_6$ _____ the number was 1.5.

N: That's the number the UN wants to $_7$ _____ the increase to. That's also the target $_8$ _____ to by many nations in the Paris Agreement. However, there's no $_9$ _____ we'll be able to prevent the temperature from rising by only that much. To do so, we need to decrease emissions by 7.6% $_{10}$ _____ between 2020 and 2030.

SELF-ASSESSMENT on CEFR-J CAN-DO Descriptor

Turn to page 7 and determine which CAN-DO Descriptor(s) you have achieved.

SDG 14: Life Below Water

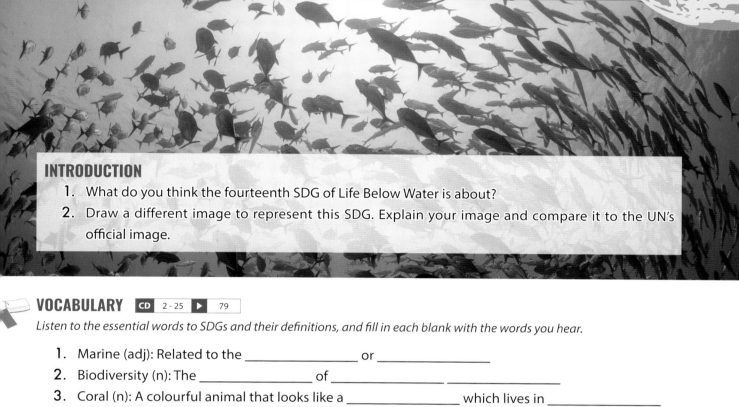

INTRODUCTION

1. What do you think the fourteenth SDG of Life Below Water is about?
2. Draw a different image to represent this SDG. Explain your image and compare it to the UN's official image.

VOCABULARY CD 2 - 25 ▶ 79

Listen to the essential words to SDGs and their definitions, and fill in each blank with the words you hear.

1. Marine (adj): Related to the _____ or _____
2. Biodiversity (n): The _____ of _____ _____
3. Coral (n): A colourful animal that looks like a _____ which lives in _____ _____
4. Acidity (n): The _____ of _____ found in something
5. Endanger (v): To _____ an _____ that is not safe
6. Pesticides (n): _____ used to kill _____
7. Unregulated (adj): Without _____ or rules for _____ or _____ use

Fill in the blanks with the correct words below.

A. Sometimes, the _____ used to protect plants from insects make other animals sick.
B. When cosmetics were an _____ industry, make up sometimes contained dangerous chemicals. Rules were needed for safety.
C. The _____ of the soil was too high for plants to grow there.
D. Do not _____ people by driving after you drink alcohol.
E. When you go snorkeling in Okinawa, do not collect the beautiful _____. Just take pictures of it instead.
F. Sharks and seaweed are both examples of _____ life.
G. Japan has a great amount of _____ from palm trees to pine trees, and from tropical fish to snow cranes.

marine   biodiversity   coral   acidity   endanger   pesticides   unregulated

READING

Q1. What do you think you will read about in terms of life below water in the reading?

Q2. Do you think life below water is important in the world right now?

Q3. How do you think the UN plans to achieve its goals related to life below water?

SDG 14: Life Below Water

CD 2-26 ▶ 80

The fourteenth SDG is "Life Below Water." The UN's goal is to protect and sustainably use the **marine** resources in our oceans, including the marine **biodiversity** of plants and animals that live below water. The jobs of over three billion people depend upon marine resources. Two hundred million of them rely on the fishing industry. However, we threaten the oceans in many ways, such
5 as overfishing and carbon dioxide emissions. By absorbing 30% of our emissions, the oceans have absorbed 90% of the excess heat that those emissions have contributed to. That heat damages **coral** and negatively affects fish that depend on coral. Marine life is also harmed by the reduction in oxygen and the increase in **acidity** that results from carbon dioxide absorption. Furthermore, we **endanger** marine life by polluting the oceans with sewage, **pesticides**, and plastics.

10 The UN is dedicated to the protection and sustainable use of our marine resources. Already, there has been an increase in protected areas of marine biodiversity from 30.5% in 2000, to 44.8% in 2015, to 46% in 2019. Furthermore, 72 countries have signed an agreement to address the problem of illegal, unreported, and **unregulated** fishing. The UN encourages more international laws related to the sustainable use and conservation of our global marine resources, such as the
15 United Nations Convention on the Law of the Sea. The UN also wants more research to be done on how to minimize and address the impacts of acidification. Moreover, by 2025, it hopes to prevent and significantly reduce marine pollution.

Words and Phrases

Read each definition and find the equivalent word used in the Passage above.

1.	T _ _ _ _ _ _ _	To cause something or someone to become vulnerable or at risk
2.	P _ _ _ _ _ _ s	Light strong materials produced by chemical processes that can be formed into shapes when heated
3.	S _ _ _ ed	To have authorized by attaching a signature
4.	R _ _ _ _ _	To trust something or someone
5.	O _ _ _ _ s	Very large seas that cover most of the Earth's surface
6.	M _ _ _ _ _ _ _	To reduce something to the lowest possible level
7.	N _ _ _ _ _ _ _ _ _	Done in such a way as to express denial, disagreement, or refusal
8.	A _ _ _ _ _ _ _ _	An arrangement, contract, or promise
9.	D _ _ _ _ _ _ _ _	Devoted
10.	C _ _ _ _ _ _ _ _ _ _ _	Preservation or protection of the natural environment and wildlife

Main Idea **Q.** Based on the reading, which one would be a suitable alternative title for SDG 14?

   a. The Problems of Overfishing

   b. Marine Biodiversity and Pollution

   c. Sustainable Use of our Marine Resources

   d. Greenhouse Gas Emissions and Ocean Acidity

Details **1.** How many people depend upon marine resources for their jobs?

   _____

2. How many people rely upon the fishing industry for their jobs?

   _____

3. What are two ways in which humans threaten the oceans?

   _____

4. How many countries signed the fishing agreement?

   _____

5. What does the UN want to do by 2025?

   _____

EXPRESS YOUR OPINION

If you were the leader of your country, how could you protect life below water?

1. *Write your opinion and its reason concisely.*


```



```

2. *Explain your opinion and its reason concisely to your classmates.*

LISTENING: Sakura's Questions About SDG 14: Life Below Water

CD 2 - Natural 27 / Slow 28 ▶ Natural 81 / Slow 82

What is Sakura going to ask her professor about SDG 14?

Listening Comprehension Questions

1st Listening

Prediction: *Listen to the dialogue and circle T (True) or F (False).*

1. [T / F] Sakura understood this SDG well before talking to Professor Swain.
2. [T / F] Sakura was surprised by the amount of plastic we use.
3. [T / F] Professor Swain apologized to Sakura for interrupting her.
4. [T / F] Acidification affects shellfish.
5. [T / F] The UN is concerned that acidification will get worse in the future.

2nd Listening

Confirmation: *Try to answer the following questions and listen to the dialogue again.*

1. How many plastic drinking bottles are bought?
   - **a.** 12 million annually
   - **b.** One million every year
   - **c.** One million every minute
   - **d.** Five trillion every year

2. What does the UN urge people to do?
   - **a.** Use as much plastic as they can
   - **b.** Organize clean ups at beaches near them
   - **c.** Interrupt organizations' use of plastic
   - **d.** Understand something about this SDG

3. What happens to shellfish?
   - **a.** They are affected by acidification.
   - **b.** They don't become as large as they should.
   - **c.** Their shells dissolve.
   - **d.** All of the above

3rd Listening

Reflection: *Listen to the part of the dialogue and fill in the blanks.*

CD 2 - Natural 29 / Slow 30 ▶ Natural 83 / Slow 84

S=Sakura Noguchi, A=Professor Alister Swain

S: I don't 1. _____ understand everything about this SDG. I mean, I get that 2. _____ plastics into the ocean is bad and 3. _____.

A: Yeah, but did you know that up to 17 million metric 4. _____ of plastic get into the ocean, 5. _____?

S: That's 6. _____ dropping!

A: Yeah, we use 7. _____ 8. _____ much plastic. The numbers are 9. _____. Globally, every minute, we buy one million plastic drinking bottles, and every year, we use five 10. _____ plastic bags.

SELF-ASSESSMENT on CEFR-J CAN-DO Descriptor

Turn to page 7 and determine which CAN-DO Descriptor(s) you have achieved.

SDG 15: Life on Land

INTRODUCTION

1. What do you think the fifteenth SDG of Life on Land is about?
2. Draw a different image to represent this SDG. Explain your image and compare it to the UN's official image.

VOCABULARY CD 2-31 ▶ 85

Listen to the essential words to SDGs and their definitions, and fill in each blank with the words you hear.

1. Deforestation (n): The process of _____ a forest by cutting it down for
   _____ or to use the land it _____

2. Acquire (v): To _____ or _____

3. Hectares (n): A unit for measuring land that is _____ to 10,000 _____
   _____

4. Drought (n): A very long time _____ _____

5. Degraded (v): Became _____ _____

6. Wildlife (n): Animals, plants, and all _____ that is found in _____

7. Restoration (n): The process of _____ something or _____ something
   _____ to its _____ condition

Fill in the blanks with the correct words below.

A. My family owns a hundred _____ of farmland in Orillia, Ontario.
B. The oil in my car _____ after six months of use, so I had to put new oil in it.
C. The _____ made the land dry, and all the plants began to die from the lack of water.
D. I love camping because I love being surrounded by _____ in a natural setting.
E. His hobby is the _____ of old cars. He has done such a great job repairing that 1958 Corvette that it looks like it is brand new.
F. _____ has many bad effects, including animals losing their places to live.
G. If you have enough money, you can _____ your own land and build a house on it.

deforestation   acquire   hectares   drought   degraded   wildlife   restoration

READING

Q1. What do you think you will read about in terms of life on land in the reading?

Q2. Do you think life on land is important in the world right now?

Q3. How do you think the UN plans to achieve its goals related to life on land?

SDG 15: Life on Land

CD 2-32 ▶ 86

The fifteenth SDG is "Life on Land." The UN's goal is to protect forests, land, and biodiversity. **Deforestation** refers to the destruction of forests for wood or to **acquire** the land. Around 1.6 billion people need forests to support themselves. Moreover, 80% of land animals, plants and insects live in forests. However, between 2010 and 2015, 3.3 million **hectares** of forest were lost to deforestation.

5 Deforestation, as well as **drought**, and the overuse of land causes land to be **degraded** until it cannot be used for farming. This process affects 74% of the poor, and 12 million hectares are lost to it annually. Both deforestation and land degradation cause the loss of biodiversity. However, biodiversity is also lost to the illegal trade of **wildlife**. Approximately 7,000 species of animals and plants are illegally sold in 120 countries.

10 The UN plans to protect forests, land, and biodiversity. It urges governments to sustainably manage forests by stopping deforestation and restoring damaged forests. It wants to raise money for developing countries, so they can sustainably manage their forests. By 2030, the UN hopes to fight land degradation by land **restoration** projects aimed at restoring land at the same rate as it is degraded. These plans to fight deforestation and land degradation will help to preserve biodiversity.

15 In addition, the UN wants global support for the prevention of illegal wildlife trade, and it wants to aid local communities, so they can sustainably manage the use of local wildlife.

Words and Phrases

Read each definition and find the equivalent word used in the Passage above.

1.	A _ _ ed _ _	Intended for
2.	S _ _ _ _ _ _	To provide people everything necessary, especially money, so that they can live
3.	L _ _ _	The state of no longer existing
4.	A _ _	To help or support in achieving something
5.	C _ _ _ _ s	To make something bad or unpleasant happen
6.	I _ _ _ _ _ _ _	Done in such a way not allowed by the law
7.	D _ _ _ _ _ _ _ _ _	The action of causing so much damage to something that it no longer exists
8.	P _ _ _ _ _ _	A series of steps or actions that lead to a result
9.	R _ _ _ _ _ _ _	Repairing something or bringing something back to its original condition
10.	A _ _ _ _ _ _ _ _ _ _ _	Roughly, about, or around

Main Idea Q. Why is the UN worried about life on land?

    a. Deforestation

    b. Land degradation

    c. Loss of biodiversity

    d. All of the above

Details 1. How many people need forests to support themselves?

_____

2. What percentage of land animals, plants, and insects live in forests?

_____

3. How many hectares of forest were lost between 2010 and 2015?

_____

4. What three things does the UN want to protect?

_____

5. What does the UN hope to do by 2030?

_____

EXPRESS YOUR OPINION

If you could immediately solve only one of the problems in the text (i.e., deforestation, loss of biodiversity, or land degradation), which one would you solve?

1. *Write your opinion and its reason concisely.*

```
┌─────────────────────────────────────────────┐
│                                             │
│                                             │
│                                             │
│                                             │
└─────────────────────────────────────────────┘
```

2. *Explain your opinion and its reason concisely to your classmates.*

LISTENING: Sakura's Questions About SDG 15: Life on Land

CD 2 - Natural 33 / Slow 34 ▶ Natural 87 / Slow 88

> What is Sakura going to ask her professor about SDG 15?

Listening Comprehension Questions

1st Listening

 Prediction: *Listen to the dialogue and circle T (True) or F (False).*

1. [T / F] Sakura read that 75% of the Earth's surface has been altered by humans.
2. [T / F] Sakura likes camping in forests.
3. [T / F] Food production has an effect on deforestation.
4. [T / F] Deforestation has no effect on biodiversity.
5. [T / F] Professor Jang thinks deforestation is the worst problem.

2nd Listening

 Confirmation: *Try to answer the following questions and listen to the dialogue again.*

1. Which statement is true?
   a. From 2015 to 2020, one million hectares of forest were destroyed.
   b. From 2015 to 2020, ten million hectares of forest were destroyed.
   c. From 2015 to 2020, ten million hectares of forest were destroyed annually.
   d. From 2015 to 2020, one million hectares of forest were destroyed annually.

2. Which statement is true?
   a. 8% of all species is threatened with extinction.   b. 40,000 species have gone extinct.
   c. 22% of animal species have gone extinct.   d. None of the above

3. Why is there still such a great loss of biodiversity?
   a. The UN isn't trying.
   b. Only 113 countries have made protecting biodiversity part of their national planning.
   c. Only 1/3 of 113 countries have made protecting biodiversity part of their national planning.
   d. Both a and c

3rd Listening

 Reflection: *Listen to the part of the dialogue and fill in the blanks.*   CD 2 - Natural 35 / Slow 36 ▶ Natural 89 / Slow 90
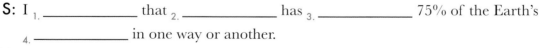
S=Sakura Noguchi, N=Professor Nina Jang

S: I $_1$. _____ that $_2$. _____ has $_3$. _____ 75% of the Earth's $_4$. _____ in one way or another.

N: That's true, and unfortunately, those changes have had some pretty $_5$. _____ effects on forests, $_6$. _____, and land quality.

S: I am sorry to hear about the forests. I love $_7$. _____ and spending time in the $_8$. _____.

N: Then, you will not be $_9$. _____ to learn that from 2015 to 2020, we $_{10}$. _____ 10 million hectares of forest per year.

SELF-ASSESSMENT on CEFR-J CAN-DO Descriptor

Turn to page 7 and determine which CAN-DO Descriptor(s) you have achieved.

SDG 16: Peace, Justice, and Strong Institutions

INTRODUCTION

1. What do you think the sixteenth SDG of Peace, Justice, and Strong Institutions is about?
2. Draw a different image to represent this SDG. Explain your image and compare it to the UN's official image.

VOCABULARY CD 2-37 ▶ 91

Listen to the essential words to SDGs and their definitions, and fill in each blank with the words you hear.

1. Conflict (n): A _____ _____ between people or groups that often _____ _____ a fight or long _____
2. Flee (v): To _____ or run away from some _____
3. Civilians (n): Regular _____ who are not _____
4. Corrupt (adj): _____ behaviour done to acquire some _____, such as money
5. Bribery (n): Giving money or gifts to people with _____ to get them to let you _____ a _____
6. Tax evasion (n): _____ _____ paying the taxes you _____ must pay
7. Cease-fire (n): An _____ to _____ fighting

Fill in the blanks with the correct words below.

A. When I was young, I watched Japanese monster movies, and I saw people _____ from Godzilla.
B. _____ do not have to wear uniforms or carry guns like soldiers do.
C. The famous American gangster Al Capone was sent to jail for _____. It is amazing that such a violent criminal only went to jail because he did not pay his taxes.
D. The _____ between North Korea and South Korea has stopped the fighting between those nations for many decades.
E. In many developing countries, _____ is the only way to get the police to help you. I can't imagine having to pay money or give presents to get a police officer to assist me.
F. A _____ over noise resulted in the two neighbours getting into a fist fight.
G. In countries with _____ police, criminals use bribery to avoid being punished for their crimes.

conflict   flee   civilians   corrupt   bribery   tax evasion   cease-fire

READING

Q1. What do you think you will read about in terms of peace, justice, and strong institutions in the reading?

Q2. Do you think peace, justice, and strong institutions are important in the world right now?

Q3. How do you think the UN plans to achieve its goals related to peace, justice, and strong institutions?

SDG 16: Peace, Justice, and Strong Institutions `CD` 2 - 38 ▶ 92

The sixteenth SDG is "Peace, Justice, and Strong Institutions." Peace means no **conflict**. Even before Russia invaded Ukraine, the UN reported that in 2019, conflicts around the world caused 79.5 million people to **flee** and killed 100 **civilians** every day. Justice refers to fair and equal treatment for everyone. In just societies, people can freely express their views without fearing harm. However, between 2010 and 2015, 1,940 journalists, human rights defenders, and union members were killed. Institutions include organizations that manage services for the public, such as government, and others that ensure laws are followed, such as the courts and police. In many countries, these institutions are disorganized and **corrupt**. Globally, that has resulted in 1 out of 4 children under age 5 not having legal birth registration, often limiting their rights and access to social services. Furthermore, weak institutions cause developing countries to lose 1.26 trillion US dollars annually due to corruption, theft, **bribery**, and **tax evasion**.

The UN wants peace, justice, and strong institutions everywhere. In March of 2020, the UN Secretary-General called for a global **cease-fire** so everyone could unite to fight COVID-19. By 2030, the UN wants to significantly reduce all forms of violence and related death rates. It also wants to end all violence against children and to ensure that everyone has birth registration. Moreover, it hopes to strengthen national and international institutions to provide justice for all, by promoting the rule of law (the principle that all people and institutions must follow the laws) everywhere.

Words and Phrases

Read each definition and find the equivalent word used in the Passage above.

1.	E _ _ _ _ _ _	To convey in words or by gestures
2.	P _ _ _ _ _ _ _ _	A rule that something is based on
3.	U _ _ _ _	A group that workers form to protect their rights
4.	F _ _ _ _ _	Done as one wishes
5.	R _ _ _ _ _ _ _ _ _ _ _	The action or process of recording something officially
6.	J _ _ _ _ _ _	The quality of being fair and reasonable
7.	I _ _ _ _ _ _ _ _ _ _ s	Organizations that specialize in something; a bank is a financial one
8.	J _ _ _ _ _ _ _ _ s	People who collect and write news stories for newspapers, magazines, radio, or television

9. S _ _ _ _ _ _ _ _ _ _   To make something stronger

10. D _ _ _ _ _ _ _ s   People who protect something

Reading Comprehension Questions

Main Idea   Q. What is SDG 16 about?

   a. Reducing the amount of conflict in the world
   b. Ensuring that people everywhere are treated equally and fairly
   c. Encouraging the improvement of organizations to promote the rule of law
   d. All of the above

Details   1. How many people fled conflicts in 2019?

   _____

2. What happened between 2010 and 2015?

   _____

3. How many children under age 5 lack birth registration?

   _____

4. How much money is lost by developing countries due to weak institutions?

   _____

5. Why did the UN Secretary-General call for a cease-fire in March of 2020?

   _____

EXPRESS YOUR OPINION

If you could speak to the leaders in a corrupt country, how could you convince them that they should follow the rule of law?

1. *Write your opinion and its reason concisely.*

┌───┐
│   │
│   │
│   │
│   │
│   │
└───┘

2. *Explain your opinion and its reason concisely to your classmates.*

LISTENING: Sakura's Questions About SDG 16: Peace, Justice, and Strong Institutions

CD 2 - Natural 39 / Slow 40 ▶ Natural 93 / Slow 94

Listening Comprehension Questions

What is Sakura going to ask her professor about SDG 16?

1st Listening

Prediction: *Listen to the dialogue and circle T (True) or F (False).*

1. [T / F] Sakura saw on TV that 79.5 million people fled conflict in 2019.
2. [T / F] Professor Swain made a comment about Ukraine invading Russia.
3. [T / F] Homicide means murder.
4. [T / F] Professor Swain argues with Sakura about justice and strong institutions.
5. [T / F] Sakura thinks SDG 16 is as important as the other SDGs.

2nd Listening

Confirmation: *Try to answer the following questions and listen to the dialogue again.*

1. Which statement is true?
   a. Professor Swain thinks the invasion of Ukraine will result in the same number of people fleeing conflict as was the case in 2019.
   b. Professor Swain thinks the invasion of Ukraine will result in a larger number of people fleeing conflict then was the case in 2019.
   c. Professor Swain thinks the invasion of Ukraine will result in a smaller number of people fleeing conflict then was the case in 2019.
   d. Professor Swain does not think that the invasion of Ukraine will result in a different number of people fleeing conflict then was the case in 2019.

2. What happened in 2018?
   a. Less people were murdered than in 2015.
   b. 440,000 people were murdered.
   c. The global homicide rate was 5.9 people per hundred thousand people.
   d. Both a and b

3. What does Sakura believe?
   a. The invasion of Ukraine was wrong.   b. Justice and strong institutions are important.
   c. SDG 16 is the most important one.   d. All of the above

3rd Listening

Reflection: *Listen to the part of the dialogue and fill in the blanks.*   **CD** 2 - Natural 41 / Slow 42 ▶ Natural 95 / Slow 96

S=Sakura Noguchi, A=Professor Alister Swain

A: It's no 1. _____ that the UN is 2. _____ about 3. _____.

S: For 4. _____. But I think 5. _____ and strong institutions are important as well.

A: No argument there, Sakura. Discrimination and corruption are serious 6. _____ to sustainable development, and we'll never root them out until strong institutions are in 7. _____ to promote the rule of 8. _____ for everyone everywhere.

S: You said it! I think that this SDG might be the most important one of them all. I really hope the UN can 9. _____ its 10. _____ by 2030.

SELF-ASSESSMENT on CEFR-J CAN-DO Descriptor

Turn to page 7 and determine which CAN-DO Descriptor(s) you have achieved.

SDG 17: Partnerships for the Goals

![photo of hands stacked together on grass]

INTRODUCTION

1. What do you think the seventeenth SDG of Partnerships for the Goals is about?
2. Draw a different image to represent this SDG. Explain your image and compare it to the UN's official image.

VOCABULARY   CD 2-43 ▶ 97

Listen to the essential words to SDGs and their definitions, and fill in each blank with the words you hear.

1. Partnerships (n): Agreements or _____ between people to do things _____ (usually for a long time)
2. Cooperative (adj): Done _____, _____ something by working with others
3. Official (adj): _____, or related to an authority such as a _____
4. Assistance (n): _____ or _____, in this case in the form of money
5. Accurately (adv): Done in a way that provides _____ _____
6. Debts (n): Amounts of money that were _____ and must be _____
7. Duties (n): An _____ cost or a tax that _____ put on _____ entering their country

Fill in the blanks with the correct words below.

A. I have a _____ roommate. He cleans our apartment in the first and third weeks of the months, and I clean it in the other weeks.
B. Students' _____ have to be paid back to banks after students graduate from school.
C. When other countries want to sell their rice in Japan, they must pay _____ on it, so their rice is more expensive than rice from Japanese farmers.
D. Many students need to get financial _____ from their parents or banks to pay for university.
E. The Canadian and Japanese prime ministers met in Ottawa to discuss _____ business.
F. If you add 2 and 2 _____, you will get an answer of 4.
G. Business _____ allow people to work together and use each other's strengths to make their companies run well.

partnerships   cooperative   official   assistance   accurately   debts   duties

READING

Q1. What do you think you will read about in terms of partnerships for the goals in the reading?

Q2. Do you think partnerships for the goals are important?

Q3. How do you think the UN plans to achieve its goals related to partnerships for the goals?

SDG 17: Partnerships for the Goals

CD 2 - 44 ▶ 98

The seventeenth SDG is "**Partnerships** for the Goals." Partnerships are **cooperative** agreements that allow people to accomplish goals together. In 2019, partnerships between developed and developing countries provided 147.4 billion dollars in **official** development **assistance** (ODA) for developing countries. This included a 1.3% increase in ODA to Africa and a 2.6% increase to the
5 lowest developed countries from 2018 to 2019. Communication between partners is essential to achieving the SDGs. However, in developing countries, only 11.2 people per 100 have access to high-speed Internet. Developing countries also need help from partners in developing systems to **accurately** measure their progress in achieving the SDGs. The lack of this data makes it harder for partners to know what other partners need.

10   The UN wants to improve the partnerships for goals. It urges developed countries to provide developing countries the money that they promised and consider giving more. Additionally, it aims to help developing countries make policies to sustainably pay their **debts**, and it hopes that developed countries will allow them not to pay some debts. Furthermore, the UN encourages developing countries to increase their exports and hopes partner countries will reduce or eliminate
15 **duties** on those goods. The UN also wants partners to provide developing countries with access to environmentally friendly technologies to develop their countries with. Moreover, by 2030, the UN intends to help developing countries create a better way of measuring their success in achieving their development goals.

Words and Phrases

Read each definition and find the equivalent word used in the Passage above.

1.	E _ _ _ _ _ s	Products or services sold abroad
2.	E _ _ _ _ _ _ _ _	Absolutely necessary; extremely important
3.	P _ _ _ _ ies	Rules or principles adopted or proposed by an organization or individual
4.	I _ _ _ _ _ s	To have a plan or purpose in one's mind
5.	D _ _ _ _ _ _ _ _ _	The process of growth or advancement
6.	M _ _ _ _ _ _	To assess or judge the effect, importance, or value of something
7.	A _ _ _ _ _ _ _ _ _ _	In addition, or also
8.	D _ _ _ _ _ _ _ _ countries	Poor countries that are trying to increase their industry and trade and improve life for their people

9. P _ _ _ _ _ _ d   To agree or pledge to do something

10. D _ _ _   Facts or statistics collected for analysis

Reading Comprehension Questions

Main Idea   Q. How do partnerships help accomplish the SDGs?

     a. Partnerships provide financial assistance for accomplishing the SDGs.
     b. Partnerships provide technological assistance for accomplishing the SDGs.
     c. Partnerships provide technical assistance for accomplishing the SDGs.
     d. All of the above

Details   1. How much ODA was provided in 2019?

    _____

2. By what percentage did the ODA to the least developed countries increase from 2018 to 2019?

    _____

3. According to the passage, what is essential to achieving the SDGs?

    _____

4. What two things does the UN want to happen in terms of the debts of developing countries?

    _____

5. What does the UN hope will happen by 2030?

    _____

EXPRESS YOUR OPINION

If you could get one company to partner with the UN to help achieve one of the SDGs, which company would you ask, and which SDG would you ask that company to help with?

1. *Write your opinion and its reason concisely.*

    [ ]

2. *Explain your opinion and its reason concisely to your classmates.*

LISTENING: Sakura's Questions About SDG 17: Partnerships for the Goals

CD 2 - Natural 45 / Slow 46 ▶ Natural 99 / Slow 100

Listening Comprehension Questions

What is Sakura going to ask her professor about SDG 17?

1st Listening

Prediction: *Listen to the dialogue and circle T (True) or F (False).*

1. [T / F] Sakura says that SDG 17 is the most important SDG.
2. [T / F] Partnerships are important for developing countries.
3. [T / F] Partnerships between countries are the only kind of partnership.
4. [T / F] A lot of money is remitted.
5. [T / F] COVID-19 will have a positive effect on remittances.

2nd Listening

Confirmation: *Try to answer the following questions and listen to the dialogue again.*

1. What information was not given?
   a. The UN wants partners in academia.
   b. The UN wants partners from show business.
   c. The UN wants regional partners.
   d. The UN wants partners from business.

2. How much money was remitted in 2019?
   a. 100 billion dollars
   b. Less money because of the jobs lost during the pandemic
   c. 554 million dollars
   d. 554 billion dollars

3. What does Sakura want to hear more about?
   a. Remittances
   b. Why Professor Jang has to run
   c. How companies can help
   d. None of the above

3rd Listening

Reflection: *Listen to the part of the dialogue and fill in the blanks.*

CD 2 - Natural 47 / Slow 48 ▶ Natural 101 / Slow 102

S=Sakura Noguchi, N=Professor Nina Jang

N: Yeah, money 1. _____ to families in developing countries from 2. _____ from those countries who work in developed countries. In 2019, 554 billion dollars was 3. _____.

S: Wow!

N: Yeah, they're a big 4. _____, but sadly the UN 5. _____ that the jobs lost in the pandemic may reduce that number by 100 billion.

S: Oh no. Are there any other 6. _____?

N: Well, the UN also 7. _____ 8. _____ with 9. _____ companies.

S: I'd love to hear 10. _____ about that.

SELF-ASSESSMENT on CEFR-J CAN-DO Descriptor

Turn to page 7 and determine which CAN-DO Descriptor(s) you have achieved.

著者

Paul G. Quinn（ポール　G．クイン）Centennial College

岡裏佳幸（おかうら　よしゆき）福岡工業大学

私たちの未来を考える—英語で学ぶＳＤＧs

2023 年 2 月 20 日　第 1 版発行
2024 年 2 月 20 日　第 3 版発行

著　　　者——Paul G. Quinn・岡裏佳幸
発　行　者——前田俊秀
発　行　所——株式会社　三修社
　　　　　　　〒 150-0001　東京都渋谷区神宮前 2-2-22
　　　　　　　TEL 03-3405-4511 / FAX 03-3405-4522
　　　　　　　振替 00190-9-72758
　　　　　　　https://www.sanshusha.co.jp
　　　　　　　編集担当　伊藤宏実

印刷・製本——日経印刷株式会社

©2023 Printed in Japan ISBN978-4-384-33516-3 C1082

表 紙 デ ザ イ ン —NON Design
本文デザイン・DTP —伊藤宏実
本 文 イ ラ ス ト —田原直子
準 拠 音 声 制 作 —高速録音株式会社
　　　　　　　　　（吹込：Howard Colefield / Jennifer Okano / MAI）

JCOPY〈出版者著作権管理機構 委託出版物〉

本書の無断複製は著作権法上での例外を除き禁じられています。複製される場合は、
そのつど事前に、出版者著作権管理機構（電話 03-5244-5088 FAX 03-5244-5089
e-mail: info@jcopy.or.jp）の許諾を得てください。

教科書準拠 CD 発売

本書の準拠 CD をご希望の方は弊社までお問い合わせください。